FORGIVENESS

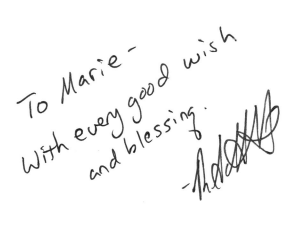

To Marie –
With every good wish
and blessing.
–Michael

FORGIVENESS
A CATHOLIC APPROACH

By R. Scott Hurd

Foreword by
Cardinal Donald Wuerl

Pauline
BOOKS & MEDIA
Boston

Library of Congress Cataloging-in-Publication Data

Hurd, R. Scott.
   Forgiveness : a Catholic approach / R. Scott Hurd ; foreword by Donald Wuerl.
       p. cm.
   ISBN 0-8198-2691-X (pbk.)
   1. Forgiveness--Religious aspects--Catholic Church. 2. Forgiveness of sin.
I. Title.
   BV4647.F55H865 2011
   241'.4--dc22
                          2011009002

Many manufacturers and sellers distinguish their products through the use of trademarks. Any trademarked designations that appear in this book are used in good faith but are not authorized by, associated with, or sponsored by the trademark owners.

Cover design by Rosana Usselmann

Cover photo: istockphoto.com

Published by Pauline Books & Media, 50 Saint Pauls Avenue, Boston, MA 02130-3491

Printed in the U.S.A.

www.pauline.org

Pauline Books & Media is the publishing house of the Daughters of St. Paul, an international congregation of women religious serving the Church with the communications media.

2 3 4 5 6 7 8 9   16 15 14 13 12

For Steph, my wife,
"God only knows where I'd be without you"

Contents

Foreword

"Courage, child, your sins are forgiven" (Mt 9:2). These powerful, consoling, healing, and restoring words addressed to the paralytic in Matthew's Gospel are directed also to each of us.

The sacrament of Reconciliation is the story of God's love that never turns away from us. God's love endures even our shortsightedness and selfishness. Like the father in the parable of the Prodigal Son, God awaits and watches and hopes for our return every time we walk away. Like the son in the same parable, all we need to do to make our way to our Father is to recognize our wrong, our need, and God's love.

But we are called to even more than the passive reception of God's mercy. Jesus asks us to be instruments of forgiveness. "Forgive us our trespasses, as we forgive those who trespass against us" (Mt 6:12). We who so generously receive the gift of God's mercy and forgiveness are expected to share as graciously with those who have offended us. In all of the petitions of the Lord's Prayer, this is the only one that carries with it a condition. We should expect our forgiveness to be measured by the gauge of our own mercy.

In *Forgiveness: A Catholic Approach*, Father R. Scott Hurd writes of the spiritual, psychological, physical, and social benefits of learning how to forgive and find peace. Drawing from his pastoral experience, in twenty-four short chapters, Father Hurd examines how human weakness affects such things as our ability to forgive and reconcile, our capacity to trust, and how we cope when a plea for forgiveness is rejected by a person we have wronged. We learn that through these very experiences, we find in Jesus Christ and the sacraments a way to move forward toward healing.

The first question Father Hurd addresses is one that perplexes many people, "Why forgive?" Here we learn that forgiveness is essential for human growth and flourishing. Forgiveness is not only a human experience, it is also an expression of God's love and mercy. Forgiveness is at once deeply personal and an opportunity for sharing the Good News. As participants in the New Evangelization, our acts of forgiveness and reconciliation offer people an experience of God's love. Father Hurd writes, "forgiveness from our hearts can turn others' hearts toward God" (see p. 20).

All of us know that there is more to forgiveness than simply saying "I'm sorry." In the section entitled, "Hallmarks of Forgiveness," Father Hurd deftly outlines seven such marks of forgiveness that reflect the teaching and example of Our Lord. In Jesus, we learn how to forgive others as God has forgiven us. Forgiveness is a decision, a process, and a gift (see p. 6).

Equally challenging today is the question of how to forgive. In *Forgiveness: A Catholic Approach* we find an entire section on this topic. With priestly wisdom, Father Hurd examines a wide variety of experiences of forgiveness and reconciliation. With examples from Scripture, Church tradition, literature, and his own ministry, he offers a useful ten-step process to aid people ready to make the decision to forgive.

As we seek to grow deeper in our understanding of the meaning of forgiveness in the Catholic tradition, this book is a welcome companion for both meditation and prayer. I am pleased to recommend *Forgiveness: A Catholic Approach* for readers looking for help in taking the first step toward forgiveness or seeking support in moving from forgiveness to reconciliation. This book is a sure guide because it so clearly, faithfully, and engagingly presents a Catholic approach to the beautiful blessing of forgiveness.

CARDINAL DONALD WUERL
Archbishop of Washington

Part I

WHY FORGIVE?

CHAPTER 1

A Lovely Idea?

"Everyone says that forgiveness is a lovely idea," wrote C. S. Lewis, "until they have something to forgive." How true that is! When we've been hurt, forgiving the one who has hurt us may be the last thing we want to do. We're angry. Forgiveness doesn't seem fair. We don't think the ones who have hurt us deserve it. We fear that forgiving them would "let them off the hook." In our pain, being told we need to forgive can seem offensive. Maybe we've been hurt often and we're just plain tired of forgiving. And that's somewhat understandable: forgiving can be a difficult and painful process that requires large doses of humility and grace. It can seem easier to stay mad or get even rather than let go and move on.

We may even conclude that forgiveness is impossible or just plain foolish. Or perhaps we've decided there are some things that never can nor should be forgiven. For instance, over half of those who responded to one survey said they would never forgive an armed robber, a rapist, or a murderer.[1] When we think this way, forgiveness is anything but a "lovely idea." It's a monstrous one!

The wisdom of Lewis's words was reinforced for me when reading comments posted in response to an Internet article about forgiveness.[2] Over and over again, hurting individuals expressed strong objections to the idea of forgiveness. One insisted that those who speak of forgiveness are "naïve" and "just don't get it." Another confessed that the article "made me sick to my stomach." A contention was made that those who speak of forgiveness have never truly been hurt themselves. If they had, they'd know that only retribution, and not forgiveness, would bring any real relief to the pain. "As time passes," the posting concluded, "the revenge factor grows."

Given the nature of the article and content of the comments, I couldn't be sure whether or not those who posted were Christian. Nevertheless, even the most committed Christians can be resistant to the idea of forgiveness, as I experienced once on a weekend retreat I led. Most of the participants had signed up for the retreat long before they knew who would be leading it or what the topic would be. Upon their arrival, as they would share with me later, many were disappointed to discover that the retreat would focus on forgiveness. Some didn't want to hear about forgiveness, because they thought the topic was too "heavy." Others thought, "This won't apply to me. I really don't have any issues with forgiveness." As the retreat unfolded, however, their attitudes changed. Many were challenged, most were inspired, and everyone learned something. They came to appreciate that perhaps they did have some forgiving to do after all.

A few realized that they needed to forgive themselves. Misconceptions about forgiveness were identified and clarified: forgiveness doesn't involve forgetting, nor does it require reconciliation or making up. Some came to admit that they really didn't know how to forgive or where to start. In the end, just about all the participants left with an understanding that they had some work to do. But they were no longer disappointed. They were grateful.

The truth is, we all have someone to forgive: from the rude driver who cut us off in traffic to the spouse who abandoned us. There's the parent who neglected us or always put us down; the friends who vanished when we needed them most; the confidant we trusted who betrayed our secret; the boss who took credit for our idea; the bully who made our school years miserable; the compassionless priest who snapped at us in the confessional; the contractor who took our money but never finished the job; the teacher who shamed us before our classmates; the back-stabbing coworker; the lover who used us; the gossiping neighbor; the lying or corrupt politician; the greedy business executive whose decisions impacted our livelihood or our environment; the ungrateful child who never calls; the racist or sexist bigot; the hypercritical mother-in-law; a violent criminal; a war-time enemy. . . . Needless to say, this is a very incomplete list.

Without exception, we've all been hurt by others; without exception, our faith invites us to forgive those who hurt us. For whatever they've done. For however many times they've done it. Even if they refuse to apologize or admit that they did anything wrong. Even if we'll never see them again, but especially if we will. We do it for ourselves. We do it for those around us and for those who've harmed us; and we do it for God, to give him glory and reveal his love to the world.

The forgiveness we're called to offer is a decision, a process, and a gift. It's a *decision* because by forgiving we choose to let go of any desire for revenge or retaliation, and we free ourselves of the bitterness and resentment that harden our hearts. Forgiveness is a *process* because letting go of resentment takes time; we may need to make the decision to forgive over and over again! Finally, forgiveness is a *gift* of love that we give freely, without expectations, exceptions, or limits. It is neither earned nor deserved. When we love the ones we forgive, we wish them happiness, not harm; well, not woe; heaven, not hell.

As always, Jesus shows us the way. He instructs us by his example, challenges us through his teaching, and forgives us from his cross. Like us, Jesus too has been hurt. He still bears the marks of that hurt in his hands, his feet, and his side. Jesus knew the betrayal of a friend and was abandoned by those he loved. He was a victim of prejudice, greed, selfishness, and cowardice. Although completely innocent, he experienced the most extreme injustice by being condemned, tortured, and executed. Yet it is he who calls us to forgive and who gives us the grace to do it. He shows us that forgiveness is not only possible, but that it is a necessity for those who would follow him. Far from being simply a "lovely idea," forgiveness is a requirement of love. Mother Teresa put it well: "If we really want to love, we must learn how to forgive."

Chapter 2

Forgive for You

Dick Fiske, an Army veteran who survived the Japanese attack on Pearl Harbor, tells of his stay in a V.A. hospital after the war.[3] He was suffering from severely bleeding ulcers, part of his stomach had been cut out, and his prospects for survival were dim.

One day a burly, cigar-chomping military doctor strolled into his room and demanded, "Sarge, what in the hell is eating at you?" "I don't know," Fiske replied, "but I think a truck ran over me." The doctor looked directly at Fiske, pointed to his gut, and said, "I can cure that, but"—as he pointed to his head—"I can't cure that." "What do you mean?" asked Fiske. "I went through your record," explained the doctor. "Good God, Sarge, who do you hate?"

It was then that the tormented veteran realized that for years he had been consumed by hate—hatred of the killing, hatred of his wartime enemies. And it was literally eating away at him, killing him from the inside out. He was living proof of the truth of an old Chinese proverb: "If you're not willing to forgive, you'd better get ready to dig two graves."

It's ironic that in refusing to forgive others, we are the ones who often wind up hurt—just as Sergeant Dick Fiske learned the hard way. But when we do forgive, we're filled with God's healing grace. Thankfully, Dick Fiske learned this lesson too. After talking with the doctor for about an hour, Fiske says that although he was bawling like a baby, it felt as if a 500-pound weight had been taken off his shoulders, and he could breathe once again. He had begun to forgive, and pain was replaced with peace. It was as Pope John Paul II wrote: "The liberating encounter with forgiveness can be experienced even by a wounded heart, thanks to the healing power of God, who is love."

Recent scientific studies confirm the healing power of forgiveness. They conclude that people who forgive live longer, healthier, and happier lives. One experiment measured the heart rate, blood pressure, and stress levels of adults who were asked to think about people who had lied to, insulted, or rejected them. Then they were given a choice. They could either imagine holding a grudge, or they could think about forgiving their offender. The results? Those who imagined forgiveness had lower heart rates and blood pressure while feeling calmer and more in control. On the other hand, those who held grudges were physically stressed, and they experienced greater feelings of anger and sadness.[4] Other studies suggest that, by not forgiving, we weaken our immune systems and place ourselves at risk for depression, a heart attack, chronic back pain, and cancer. Even our memory and the ability to think straight are compromised.[5]

Failing to forgive can ruin not only our health, but also our relationships. When we fail to forgive a hurt, we can become fearful of being hurt again. So we retreat into a shell and keep others at a distance, because we have a hard time trusting them. We wind up feeling not only angry, but also very much alone. At the same time, misery usually loves company. We want to share our bitterness with others. Our resentment spreads, affecting more and more people within our sphere of relationships, making us difficult to love. We drive people away. Or, if they can't get away, we drive them crazy.

Our misery may even come to define us; our identity will become one with our hurt. We'll be known as the cheated spouse, the unappreciated child, the wronged employee, the victim to be pitied. At one level, we might even like this, because it allows us to get sympathy by playing the martyr. We may become proud, self-righteous, and holier-than-thou, because we feel morally superior to the person who hurt us. What's more, we may enjoy looking good at their expense: we're the "good guy," and they're the "bad guy." And to make sure that others know this, we gossip, slandering the one who has harmed us far and wide.

When we forgive, we shed this identity. We may fear losing it, because we've become so comfortable with it. If so, we need to take a step back and look at who we've become. Is that really who we want to be? Is that really a person others would want to be with? In both cases, the answer is probably "No!"

It's certainly not who God wants us to be. God wants us to be healthy, happy people. Jesus came that we might have life—and have life in abundance! By failing to forgive, we deny ourselves the abundant life Jesus invites us to share. We also deny ourselves God's forgiveness. Think about what we pray in the Our Father: "Forgive us our trespasses, as we forgive those who trespass against us." God's forgiveness cannot enter an unforgiving heart. A priest friend of mine says, only half-jokingly, that when we meet Jesus face to face at the end of our lives, he'll appear as our worst enemy. Why? Because our enemy is the measure of our forgiveness. If we're not willing to forgive an enemy, how can we expect Jesus to forgive us?

When we've been offended, we suffer. By not forgiving, we only add to our suffering; we rub salt into our own wound. Not forgiving hurts us physically, relationally, and spiritually. We become miserable; we make others miserable; we push God away. We may even, like Sergeant Dick Fiske, quite literally be killing ourselves.

As Charles Dickens wrote, "Without a willingness to forgive those who have hurt us, it is not likely that our lives can go on in any meaningful manner." But we all want to live meaningful lives. We all want to be healed of our pain. We want to be happy, and we want to be loved instead of pitied. We want to be close to God. That's why forgiving is so essential for us.

CHAPTER 3

Forgive for Others

In eastern Africa, ethnic Hutus and Tutsis have coexisted for centuries. But in 1994, violence erupted between them, leaving 800,000 people dead, mostly in Rwanda. Women, children, and the aged were brutally massacred, often by child soldiers. The fabric of society was completely torn apart.

One survivor of this unspeakable tragedy was Dativa Nyangezi Ngaboyisonga.[6] When the violence came to her neighborhood, she and a crowd of others sought refuge in a church. The church wasn't large enough to accommodate everyone, so she allowed two relatives to enter while she remained outside. That decision probably saved her life. The attackers focused upon the church, shooting and throwing hand grenades inside. Dativa fled for safety. Hiding in a jungle, she survived a snake attack and being captured by soldiers, who tortured and killed her father and an aunt in front of her. In her desperation, she made a promise to God. "If you spare me," she begged, "I'll do whatever you want. I will serve you and even try to serve these people." By "these people," she meant her attackers.

God heard her prayer, Dativa firmly believes, and since then she's kept her part of the bargain. After the violence ended, a religious sister asked Dativa to serve as an interpreter for imprisoned child soldiers. Dativa agreed, and she found herself caring for hundreds of youth who came to call her "Mama." She taught them about the love of God and the importance of forgiveness. The child soldiers would ultimately be released to their families. Dativa would ultimately become prison superintendent.

Dativa forgave her attackers and all those who had subjected her people to hatred and violence. She did so, not only for herself, but also for them and, indeed, for her whole nation. "It's possible to change their hearts," she said. "We have to build a society and try to rise above [the violence]." Her efforts and the efforts of those like her have borne much fruit. There are now entire villages in Rwanda where killers and victims' families live side by side in peace.

When we forgive others, we benefit ourselves. As with Dativa Nyangezi Ngaboyisonga, we also may benefit those we forgive. For instance, it may be that those who have hurt us are terribly sorry for what they've done. They're wracked by guilt and wish that they could reverse the hands of time and undo what they did. If we forgive them, we release them from their prison of regret and shame. Should we be in a relationship with them, our forgiveness can bring healing and hope for a better future. By refusing to forgive, on the other hand, we keep those who've hurt us locked in prison. We may even do this intentionally, as a way of punishing. We purposely deny them peace. We deny ourselves peace as well. By extension, we also deny peace to those around us. When we fail to forgive, we're likely to become embittered, cynical, resentful people. We create a climate of negativity around us. Misery loves company, and our misery will make our company miserable too, before it drives others away. And those who can't get away, such as members of our family, may "catch" our misery. Misery is infectious; it can spread like a cancer. Pope John Paul II put it very well: "What sufferings are inflicted on humanity," he exclaimed, "because of the failure . . . to forgive."

It's especially important that we forgive for the sake of our families. Our failing to forgive a spouse, an ex-spouse, a relative, or an in-law can shatter a family's cohesion or, if it's already been shattered, prevent some of the pieces from being put back together again. We force people to "take sides." We slander, gossip, and even sabotage attempts at peacemaking. We drive wedges between those who once may have been close. Holidays and big events like weddings or graduations become occasions of anxiety and dread instead of togetherness and joy. Kids sense the tension and become agitated or withdrawn. And they pick up our bad lessons and come to follow our example.

We need to model forgiveness for children in particular, so they can grow into forgiving adults. Forgiveness doesn't come naturally to us. Like love, it needs to be learned. Most of all, it needs to be learned at home.

That's why the *Catechism of the Catholic Church* (no. 1657) describes the family as a "school" of forgiveness.

I've witnessed the truth of this at a retreat I've attended with my family for several summers. One entire day is devoted to forgiveness. After a morning presentation, everyone writes a letter to each member of his or her family, asking forgiveness for things he or she has done. In the evening, at a special ceremony, the letters are exchanged. Siblings apologize to their brothers and sisters. Spouses apologize to each other. Children apologize to their parents. Parents apologize to their children. Tears are shed and hugs are given. It's a powerful experience. And it's an equally powerful lesson for everyone involved.

It's not only children who need to be taught forgiveness, however. Our world is filled with people who have never experienced forgiveness, have never learned how to forgive, or who are convinced that forgiveness is either pointless or impossible. By being forgiving people, we can show them otherwise. We demonstrate how and why to forgive; we witness that forgiveness is not only possible, it is also essential.

Imagine what life would be like if we all forgave one another. It would be heavenly, wouldn't it? But the sad reality is that this is not going to happen. Human nature and human history indicate that there will always be enmity, hatred, revenge, and mercilessness in our world. Such things are inevitable this side of heaven. It's not inevitable, however, that we contribute to them. That's why Jesus calls us to create a little bit of heaven here on earth by extending forgiveness and promoting peace for ourselves, for those around us, for the whole human race.

When we forgive, we shine the light of Christ's love into a darkened world, and we bear witness to the truth that love is stronger than hate.

Chapter 4

Forgive for God

A teacher stares over the shoulder of a child, busily working at a desk. "What are you doing?" asks the teacher. "Drawing a picture of God," replies the student. The teacher protests: "But nobody knows what God looks like!" "They will when I'm done!" quips the youngster with a mischievous smile.

If you were asked to draw a picture of God, what would yours look like? Would you portray God as smiling, or would he instead be wearing a frown? I ask this because too many people imagine God to be unhappy, even angry. In their minds, God is easily offended and eager to punish. For them every day is an audition with God. Their life of faith is filled with more fear and uncertainty than it is with hope and peace. To walk with God is to walk on eggshells. Confession isn't a joy-filled reconciliation of a friendship, but a stay of execution.

Where do we get such an image of God? Possibly from our parents. As children, our image of God is greatly shaped through the messages sent by Mom and Dad and their vision of the world. If they never spare the rod, we'll grow up thinking that God won't spare the rod either. Unaffectionate, unreasonable, or unavailable parents give their kids the impression that God is more of the same. Our religious upbringing can also establish a skewed image of God. If we were taught to understand ourselves as "sinners in the hands of an angry God," how could we help but think of God as anything but angry? In addition, tough and painful life experiences can shape our image of God. Our asking, "Why did God let this happen to me?" can easily become, "What kind of God would let this happen?" And if we don't know God too well, we might conclude: not a very nice one. We can be scared into obeying this "god." Unfortunately, he's difficult to love, because he doesn't seem very loving, let alone lovable.

But is this how God wants us to think of him? Not at all. He's always trying to set the record straight, and whenever he gets a "bad rap," he calls upon us to get the true story out. That was the experience of St. John Bosco. As a child, he dreamed that he was surrounded by misbehaving and foul-mouthed boys. John tried to stop them by shouting and fighting, but was unsuccessful. Then a man with a shining face and a flowing robe made John the leader of the boys and said, "You will have to win these friends of yours not with blows, but with gentleness and kindness." As an adult, John took these words to heart in his work with poor and neglected children.

John founded two religious orders to assist him. Contrary to the methods of discipline at the time, he forbade spanking or any form of corporal punishment, and he stressed the importance of being joyful, friendly, kind, and patient with children. Young people should be treated that way, he taught, because this is how Jesus treats all of us. He wrote, "[Jesus] treated sinners with a kindness and affection that caused some to be shocked, others to be scandalized, and still others to hope for God's mercy."

By being people who forgive, we too can give others hope for God's mercy. We can help paint for them an accurate picture of God—God as revealed in Jesus. Just as St. John Bosco gave witness to youth of a God of love rather than a "god" of punishment, we manifest God's nature to others whenever we forgive. By forgiving, we proclaim a forgiving and merciful God. Forgiveness is an act of evangelization; it's a way we can share the good news of the Gospel.

By forgiving, we declare God's goodness to the world. We show those who doubt God's forgiveness the truth of who God really is. Even more, we touch those we forgive with the finger of God. As Christians, we are not simply followers of Christ. We are the "body of Christ," the Church, through which Christ's presence is extended in the world today. As is said so beautifully in words attributed to St. Teresa of Avila, "Christ has no body now on earth but yours, no hands but yours, no feet but yours. Yours are the eyes through which Christ's compassion is to look out to the earth; yours are the feet by which he is to go about doing good; and yours are the hands by which he is to bless us now." To which we might add: ours are the hearts that share his mercy.

Our forgiveness can inspire not only those who imagine God to be angry and unhappy, but it can also inspire those who can't imagine that God exists at all! Forgiveness from our hearts can turn others' hearts toward God. We acknowledge this every Good Friday as we commemorate Jesus's crucifixion. The special prayers for that day's liturgy include a petition "for those who do not believe in God." In it, we ask God that all may "recognize in the lives of Christians the tokens of your love and mercy, and gladly acknowledge you as the one true God and Father of us all." One such token that we can offer is forgiveness.

To know me is to love me, it's often said, and that's supremely true of God. Yet so many don't know God. Either they don't know of God, they don't think there is a God to know, or what they think they know of God is wrong. Yet, God wants them to know him and to love him, because he knows and loves them, just as he knows and loves us. And God calls us to let him love those who don't know him through the forgiveness we share. Should we answer that call, we make God's forgiveness, and his love, very real. As the *Catechism of the Catholic Church* (no. 2843) emphasizes, when we do this, "the Lord's words on forgiveness, the love that loves to the end, become a living reality."

PART II

HALLMARKS
OF FORGIVENESS

CHAPTER 5

No Fair!

An acquaintance of mine and his father sat down together to watch *The Scarlet and the Black*, a movie about Monsignor Hugh O'Flaherty, a courageous Irish priest who, while working at the Vatican during the Second World War, helped hide thousands of refugees from the Nazis. Colonel Herbert Kappler, the local Gestapo chief, tried in vain to have the priest assassinated. When the Allies occupied Rome, however, and Kappler was taken into custody, O'Flaherty helped Kappler's wife and children, and he visited Kappler in jail on a regular basis. Thanks to O'Flaherty's demonstration of Christian love, Kappler converted to Catholicism.

At the end of the movie, a text appeared on the screen with an appeal for forgiveness. When my acquaintance's father saw this, he absolutely hit the roof. He was a veteran who had fought the Nazis, and he had decided long ago that under no circumstances would he *ever* forgive them. They had done too much harm, he explained, and committed too much evil. To forgive them would be wrong, he insisted, because *it wouldn't be fair.*

He is absolutely right. It wouldn't be fair for him to forgive the Nazis. But there's nothing fair about forgiveness. When we've been hurt, it's typical for us to want to retaliate, to get even. We want those who've hurt us to know how we feel and to get a taste of their own medicine. We think: they've hurt us, we should be able to hurt them back! After all, *it's only fair.*

Strict justice is fair, but forgiveness is not. God himself isn't fair. That sounds strange, I realize. So often, life doesn't seem fair. Bad things happen to good people. Good things happen to bad people. The rich get richer and the poor get poorer. We assume that, in contrast to all this unfairness, surely God must be fair! Yet God isn't fair. That's because there's a difference between what we might call human fairness, or human justice, and the justice of God.

Human justice is about people getting what they deserve. With human justice an "eye for an eye" is fair. But as both Martin Luther King and Mahatma Gandhi remind us, an "eye for an eye" mentality leaves everybody blind! Thankfully, God's justice is different. The liturgy of the Twenty-fifth Sunday of Ordinary Time puts it beautifully: "The perfection of justice is found in [God's] love." In other words, God's justice is about love, and love is about giving of oneself for the good of others. Love isn't concerned with getting what we think we deserve; it isn't preoccupied with our so-called fair share. Instead, true love gives without counting the cost.

It is this love, this divine justice, that we as Christians are called to offer those who hurt us. Yet so often we fall short of this standard, all in the name of fairness. We withhold forgiveness because we think it's not fair; or we restrict our forgiveness with a "three strikes and you're out" mentality, which is really probation and not forgiveness at all. We'll even hope to see others suffer harm because we think they deserve it. The Bible tells the story of Jonah, whom God wanted to preach repentance to the sinful people of Nineveh. Jonah, however, would have preferred to see them destroyed rather than saved. At first, Jonah tried to run away from God. When that didn't work, Jonah reluctantly preached to the Ninevites. When they listened and changed their ways, however, Jonah became angry. He knew they would be spared the destruction he thought they deserved. Jonah complained: "I knew that you are a gracious and merciful God, slow to anger, and abounding in steadfast love, and ready to relent from punishing" (Jon 4:2). God had to remind Jonah that in his love, justice is always tempered by mercy, and that while he may indeed hate the sin, he always loves the sinner.

Like Jonah, sometimes we too want to see others get what we think they deserve. We want to see strict justice done. We want fairness! Thank God that God isn't fair with us. God doesn't give us what we deserve. God is merciful, and he forgives. He asks us to do the same, not in the name of fairness, but in the name of love.

Jesus tells a parable of a servant who was in debt to his king (Mt 18:23–35). Specifically, the servant owed "ten thousand talents." A talent was equivalent to six thousand days' wages for a typical laborer. To earn ten thousand talents, a laborer would need to work every day, without rest, for nearly 200,000 years![7] Jesus's point is that this particular servant owed an amount impossible to pay off. Nevertheless, the "compassionate" king in the parable forgave the servant's debt. But when that servant came upon a fellow servant who owed him a tiny amount, he threatened him, choked him, and had him thrown into prison. When the king learned of this, he was terribly angry. He said, "Should you not have had pity on your fellow servant, as I had pity on you?" (Mt 18:33).

Jesus speaks these same words to us. He calls us to forgive others as we have been forgiven by him. He knows that it's not fair. Life certainly wasn't fair to him. Friends betrayed him. Loved ones rejected him. The government and organized religion turned their backs on him, and even though he was completely innocent, he was sentenced to death, tortured, and executed. He still bears the marks of that experience. Yet, he still forgives, as can we. "We can stop forgiving others," a roadside church sign proclaimed, "as soon as God stops forgiving us."

CHAPTER 6

No Exceptions

Following the horrible terrorist attacks of September 11, 2001, one prominent American politician warned the terrorists: "God may have mercy on you, but we won't!" This statement reflected the anger and attitude of many Americans during that difficult time. People wanted revenge and retaliation; mercy and forgiveness were out of the question.

It's not uncommon for us to place limits and restrictions on who we think are candidates for forgiveness. Many people insist that they would never forgive a violent criminal. Husbands and wives insist that they'd never forgive their spouse if he or she were unfaithful. In *The Sunflower,* concentration camp survivor Simon Wiesenthal invited readers to consider what they would do if asked, as he was, for forgiveness from a dying member of the SS. In response, author Cynthia Ozick wrote: "Forgiveness is pitiless. It forgets the victim. It blurs over suffering and death. It drowns out the past.

The face of forgiveness is mild, but how stony to the slaughtered . . . Let the SS man . . . go to hell."[8]

Sometimes we Catholics can be just as unforgiving as anyone else. A Franciscan friend of mine, Father Jude Winkler, tells a story to illustrate this. There are two lines leading to heaven. Standing in the first, longer line are mostly decent, churchgoing folk. The other line is much shorter, and it includes some surprising figures: Genghis Kahn, Caligula, Idi Amin, Joseph Stalin, and other equally unsavory characters. What's even more shocking is that this line is moving faster than the longer one! Seeing this, the churchgoing folk begin to gripe and complain. "If we'd known that people like *that* were going to get in," they grumble, "we'd have had a lot more fun while we were alive!" Just then, Jesus appears. "I'm sorry," he says, "but I thought you lived the way you did because you loved me. And if you really did love me, you'd be happy that I forgave these other people!" Then he shuts the door.

This is an intentionally provocative story, and it's not meant to suggest that Stalin or Hitler or anyone else is necessarily in heaven. That's God's decision, not ours. What this story is meant to suggest, however, is that Catholics can at times be unforgiving, in spite of the example of Jesus and the teaching of the Church. Jesus offers forgiveness to everyone, and he invites us to do the same, regardless of what they have done—even if what they did was monstrously evil. As Dominican Father Peter Cameron has written, "Christian forgiveness is not occasional or optional. Forgiveness does not concern itself merely with minor, manageable transgressions, but specifically with monumental ones. That is why, as one of the culminating acts of his earthly ministry, Jesus from the cross asks forgiveness precisely for the people who murder him."9

Jesus came not to condemn the world, but to save it. He actually seeks out sinners to forgive and heal, much as a good shepherd would search high and low for a lost sheep. During his lifetime, Jesus was often criticized for associating with people who were publicly labeled as sinners. Not surprisingly, many such sinners became Jesus's followers. They still do today.

Jesus places no limits or conditions on the forgiveness he offers to us. That's the model for the forgiveness we're to offer others. Once, a mother and her adult daughter found themselves in a heated argument. At one point, the daughter apologized for what she had said and done, and she asked her mother's forgiveness. Her mother hesitated, seemingly reluctant to forgive. The daughter sensed this and asked, "Don't you think that if I told Jesus I was sorry, he'd forgive me?" Her mother, however, was unmoved. "I don't presume to say what Jesus would or would not do," she said.

It's true that the Lord's ways are oftentimes a mystery to us. His ways are not our ways, nor his thoughts our thoughts. That's why it might be prudent for us not to presume to say what Jesus might or might not do in certain circumstances. But when it comes to forgiveness, we can say with absolute certainty what Jesus would do. Jesus offers his forgiveness anytime, anywhere, and to any person, even the moment before death. An old English rhyme recalls how a rider asks for and receives God's mercy as he falls from his horse to his death: "Betwixt the stirrup and the ground, mercy I asked, mercy I found."

Maybe those who insist that they *would* never forgive a murderer, a rapist, or an armed robber, really mean that they *could* never forgive such a person. Perhaps we feel that way. Radical forgiveness like that, we may conclude, is possible only for great saints or exceptionally holy people. Not ordinary folk like us. Forgive a murderer, a terrorist, a Nazi prison guard? We could never do that! Or so we might think. But Jesus says to us: "Yes, you can." He doesn't call us to do things that are impossible. If we couldn't forgive such people, Jesus wouldn't insist that we do so. He doesn't set us up for failure.

"To be a Christian," wrote C. S. Lewis, "means to forgive the inexcusable, because God has forgiven the inexcusable in you." In other words, our forgiveness needs to be unlimited. After all, Jesus's forgiveness to us has no limits! Neither does his love. There may be times we feel like saying, "God may have mercy on you, but I won't!" But as Christians, what we can say instead is: "Because God has mercy on you, so will I."

CHAPTER 7

No Strings Attached

"You've Been Pre-Forgiven: Open to Find out How!" proclaimed the envelope in my mailbox. Inside was a pitch from an auto insurance company. It depicted a license plate that read "4 GIVN." "For your first accident," it explained, "your premium won't go up—not even a penny." Nothing was said, however, about a second accident. Presumably, there'd be no "forgiveness" for that.

Placing limits on "accident forgiveness," as it's called, makes sense for an insurance company. Unfortunately, we often want to place limits on the forgiveness we offer to those who hurt us. We might be willing to forgive a first offence, and maybe even a second. But a third? It's "three strikes, and you're out."

At other times we want to establish preconditions before we're willing to forgive. In *Juiced*, a tell-all book by baseball's Jose Canseco, fellow player Rafael Palmiero was fingered for using illegal steroids. Palmiero's reputation was ruined, and he was forced to testify to Congress. In response, Palmiero had this to say: "If it turns out to be a positive thing that he wrote this stupid book, and he turns himself around and can be a positive role model, I'll forgive him." [10] The first word in Palmiero's statement —"If"—is key. Palmiero was willing to forgive, but only *if* his terms were met.

Far too often we think forgiveness is something that must be earned. We're all familiar with the cliché of a husband walking through the front door with a bouquet of flowers. His wife, however, isn't fooled. She demands, "Okay, what have you done?" Her assumption is that he's done something wrong, and that his flowers are a bribe for forgiveness.

But is this the way it is with God? A woman anoints Jesus's feet with expensive ointment as tears stream down her face (Lk 7:36–50). Jesus assures her that her sins, which were many, are forgiven. Was her gift a bribe? No. Jesus makes it clear that it is on account of her faith, and not her gift, that she is forgiven.

True forgiveness, like love, cannot be bought with money or bribery. Otherwise forgiveness would simply be a ransom and not a free gift. And that would mean that only those who were able to pay could hope to be forgiven. But God knows there's no way for us to pay the price for our sins. Thankfully, God is not an extortionist or a loan shark. He is our loving Father who would never demand that we pay an impossible price. Jesus his Son paid the price for us on the cross. In light of this, we might say that our forgiveness came at a cost! For us, however, it comes free.

Sometimes we need to be reassured of this, because it seems just too good to be true. This was the case with an elderly woman who made her confession with me before a serious, risky surgery. When she received absolution, she was filled with joy and peace. But as she left, she turned to me and said, "Father, I don't feel as if I deserve God's forgiveness." "Of course you don't. None of us deserve it," I replied. "Forgiveness is a free gift from God."

We might protest this, however, and say: "Doesn't God set conditions on our receiving his forgiveness?" After all, Jesus taught us to pray, "Forgive us our trespasses, as we forgive those who trespass against us." Surely this means that God forgives us *only* if we forgive others! It sounds as if he takes a "wait and see" attitude. But that's not the case. God's love is unconditional, and, therefore, his forgiveness is too. His forgiveness is a gift of grace, and grace is always free. But since it's a gift, not everyone will wish to accept it. God won't force it upon us. It's always there for the taking. Yet, if we don't forgive others, our hearts become hard, and God's forgiveness can't enter in. By refusing to forgive, we in turn refuse God's forgiveness. That's why St. Francis of Assisi could write, "It is in pardoning that we are pardoned."

God doesn't make us pay for our forgiveness. He doesn't set limits on how many times we may be forgiven. There are no preconditions, no fine print, no strings attached. But can we say that about the forgiveness we have to offer? So often we extend forgiveness like banks extend credit. To get a loan, we must first prove that we're creditworthy. Then a credit limit is established that we can't exceed. And if we don't honor the agreement, the credit is withdrawn. At the very least,

there's a penalty! So too with our forgiveness. We delay
it until we believe the persons who have hurt us are worthy of it, or if we think they've shown that they're truly
sorry. Sometimes we withhold it in hopes of punishing
the other person, or making him or her feel ashamed. We
set conditions. We establish limits. We demand an apology. And when we do offer forgiveness, it's given with
the expectation that the other person will change.

Jesus does none of these things. He never waits for an
apology. In fact, he never mentions that in his teaching.
He doesn't withhold forgiveness, delay it, or set limits on
it. Peter asks Jesus how many times we should forgive
another: "Seven times?" Jesus replies: "Seventy times
seven times!" (Mt 18:22). We're not to take that too literally. Seventy times seven is only 490. If that were the
upper limit, most marriages wouldn't last! And it would
suggest that we should keep score. That's the last thing
Jesus wants us to do.

To understand what Jesus meant, we need to appreciate that seven was considered a perfect number. In the
Bible, the number was often associated with God. By
saying we need to forgive seventy times seven times, Jesus
is stressing that our forgiveness needs to be like God's:
generous, without conditions, without limits, without
waiting, and, above all, free. Such forgiveness—true forgiveness—is a gift. Then again, we should know that by
its name: For-*give*.

Chapter 8

Forgive and Forget?

Along with "God helps those who help themselves" and "cleanliness is next to godliness," "forgive and forget" is one of those lines that many people mistakenly think is in the Bible. The Bible does say a great deal about forgiveness, but nowhere does it say that forgiveness requires us to forget. In fact, the origins of "forgive and forget" are words spoken by Don Quixote to his sidekick Sancho Panza.

"Forgive and forget" may sound noble. Unfortunately, it's just not realistic. If we try to do it, we'll be as unsuccessful as Don Quixote was at jousting with windmills. Our memories aren't computer disks that can simply be wiped clean. Our minds don't come equipped with a delete button. When we've been hurt by someone, especially seriously, it's unlikely that we'll ever forget the trauma. We actually shouldn't completely forget such things. The memory might keep us from placing ourselves in a similar situation in the future, or lead us to avoid a dangerous person who might hurt us again. As has often been said, those who forget the lessons of history are doomed to repeat them.

Nevertheless, because there's a popular conception that we need to forget in order to forgive, we sometimes go to great lengths to do so, and we beat ourselves up when we find we can't. We think we've failed; we feel ashamed. True, it is possible to forget the little things that are done to us. Memories fade with time. But trying to forgive and forget a serious hurt is setting ourselves up for disappointment, because it's impossible to achieve. As the *Catechism of the Catholic Church* teaches: "It is not in our power not to feel or to forget an offense" (no. 2843). We might be able to repress a painful memory, but that doesn't solve the problem—it only buries it. Repressed memories fester, and they always come bubbling back up.

At times it's essential that we remember what has happened to us. However, this doesn't mean that we should "keep score" in our relationships by keeping track of every offense. As St. Paul wrote, love "doesn't keep a record of wrongs that others do" (1 Cor 13:5, CEV). Nevertheless, we often do this. We use this record to justify our anger when we argue and fight. Relationship counselors call this "kitchen sinking." Instead of focusing on the matter at hand, we bring up incidents from the past to shame the one we're arguing with. "And another thing . . ." we shout, "don't you remember when you. . . ." We throw all our past hurts into the kitchen sink. When we do this we're not trying to resolve a problem, we're trying to beat down the other person. That's not "fighting fair." It reveals that we haven't forgotten. It also reveals that we've yet to forgive.

By holding on to our hurts, we hold them over the head of the one who hurt us. The expression "hold it over their head" comes from an ancient Greek legend about Damocles, who today might be called a bootlicker. He tried to impress Dionysius, the ruler of Syracuse, by telling him how great he was because of his power and authority. When Dionysius offered to trade places with him for a day, Damocles quickly accepted. Damocles enjoyed the experience until he sat at a banquet that evening, looked up, and saw a sharpened sword hanging over his head, held aloft by a single horsehair. Damocles changed his mind about Dionysius on the spot. He realized that Dionysius, because of his position, lived in constant fear.

When we fail to forgive others, we place a "sword of Damocles" over their heads. One little misstep on their part will break the horsehair and unleash the sword of our anger. We put the others in fear of our wrath. We haven't forgotten what they've done, which is normal. But we've let our memories become a weapon.

Forgiveness may not require forgetting, but it does require letting go. It involves putting the matter behind us and not letting it continue to be an issue for us. We're no longer filled with resentment and bitterness. No more do we desire revenge. We don't pull it out of our pocket as a trump card when we argue. We don't use the memory in a manipulative way. Instead, it's done. It's over. Not forgotten, but forgiven.

Before they were saints, the seventeenth-century French nun St. Margaret Mary Alacoque shared with her confessor, St. Claude de la Columbière, that she was receiving visions of the Sacred Heart of Jesus. St. Claude was skeptical, so he directed St. Margaret Mary to ask Jesus, the next time he appeared, what Claude had said during his last confession. When she did ask Jesus what sins Claude had confessed, Jesus responded: "I forget." As Son of God, it's of course not really possible for Jesus to forget. He knows everything! But he can wipe our slates clean. When he forgives, it's as if he forgets, because he no longer holds our sins against us. They're in the past, and that's where they stay.

Management gurus insist that remaining stuck in the past is rarely a recipe for business success. Those who focus on the future succeed. That's also true for relationships and the spiritual life. If we remain stuck in the past by clinging to past wounds, we embitter ourselves and hurt others. That's one reason Jesus said that those who put their hands to the plow but keep looking back are not fit for the kingdom of God (see Lk 9:62)! Jesus knows that we can't forgive and forget, but he calls us to forgive and let go, so we're not looking back in bitterness, but moving forward in faith.

CHAPTER 9

Don't Be a Doormat

Several years ago, I gave a series of talks at a parish about forgiveness. One evening, I spoke about how Jesus taught us to forgive those who hurt us "seventy times seven times." When I was through, a woman raised her hand with a question. She was worried that following Jesus's teaching would make a person vulnerable to abuse. She thought that forgiving a person for hurting us repeatedly actually invited them to hurt us again. I couldn't help but wonder if she, or someone close to her, had been a victim of domestic violence.

I was grateful that she shared her concern. Domestic violence is widespread in our society. It includes not only physical harm, but also sexual, psychological, verbal, and economic abuse. A common pattern in abusive relationships is for a man (although sometimes a woman) who has committed domestic violence to ask forgiveness, and to promise never to do it again. The woman forgives him, but later he commits another act of violence. This cycle of forgiveness and abuse may go on for quite some time. If the victim is a married Christian, she may believe that forgiving an abusive husband requires staying with him, and that leaving would betray her wedding vows. She may think she's at fault, or even that she's being punished by God. She's suffering as Jesus suffered, she may conclude. Isn't enduring that suffering the loving, Christian thing to do?

Jesus does want us to be generous in forgiving. That doesn't mean, however, that he wants us to be a doormat or a punching bag. As Christians, at times we are called upon to carry a cross, to suffer, but we don't have to suffer unnecessarily, as with domestic violence. Jesus himself did not suffer unnecessarily. On many occasions he avoided being hurt or abused. When he was a newborn, Mary and Joseph fled the country to protect Jesus from being killed by Herod's soldiers. The Gospels reveal that at times people tried to stone him or throw him off a cliff, but Jesus got away. Jesus avoided certain places where he knew that people were hostile to him. He taught his disciples to shake the dust from their feet and leave those towns that rejected their ministry. Jesus removed himself from dangerous situations many times.

He did suffer horribly, of course, but only when it was necessary to fulfill his Father's will. As he traveled to Jerusalem, Jesus explained to his apostles that he would need to suffer to "accomplish his purpose" of dying and rising, so that we could be forgiven. For him to do this, he continued, he would need to suffer at the right place— Jerusalem—and at the right time, "not today, tomorrow, and the following day" (Lk 13:31–33). Until that day arrived, he avoided any suffering that would keep him from fulfilling his mission.

As Jesus's example makes clear, there's a difference between necessary and unnecessary suffering. Necessary suffering springs from our loving choices to help others or ourselves become the people God created us to be. Unnecessary suffering simply makes us victims of another's illness or sin. It's been said that love without suffering is sentimentality, but not all suffering is consistent with love.

There are times when you and I, in imitation of Jesus, need to avoid or end hurtful situations in which we would suffer unnecessarily. After all, while Jesus insisted that we are to love our neighbors, he also stressed that we're to love ourselves. Stopping hurtful behavior is one way we love ourselves. It's okay to say no to those who would hurt us. Depending on the circumstances, we may need to draw the line and say, "enough is enough," put our foot down, blow the whistle, change jobs, leave the house, distance ourselves, defend ourselves or others, maybe even end a relationship.

Love may require that we protect ourselves or stand up for ourselves. Forgiveness doesn't preclude challenging the behavior of those who are harming us. For our own good (not to mention the other person's!), hurtful behavior needs to be addressed.

Yet sometimes we avoid standing up for ourselves because we find it easier just to "let things slide." We don't want to rock the boat, because we're trying to keep the peace. Instead of peace, however, what results are hurt feelings, resentments, broken hearts, troubled consciences, migraines, and ulcers. It has been said that only driftwood goes with the flow.

It's true that Jesus did teach us to "turn the other cheek." But what he was referring to is avoiding retaliation—the act of returning evil for evil. Protecting ourselves, however, is in no way evil. The intent is not to hurt the other person, but to keep ourselves from being hurt.

People who hurt us are always worthy of our forgiveness, but they may no longer be worthy of our trust. "I forgive you" is not the same as "That's okay," or "Don't worry about it," or "It's nothing." If we've been hurt, that *is* something. It's not okay. Forgiveness isn't a denial of our pain. Forgiveness doesn't condone what's been done to us or pretend that nothing happened, and it doesn't let the persons who hurt us off the hook. They're still accountable, and responsible, for their actions. Pope John Paul II forgave Mehmet Ali Agca, who tried to assassinate him with a handgun. Nevertheless, Agca remained in prison. Violent criminals can't stay on the street; they're too dangerous. In a similar way, dishonest or disruptive people can't stay on the job. They can't be trusted! They can, however, be forgiven.

It's often said that forgiveness is for wimps, those who don't have the power or courage to defend themselves. Jesus shows us otherwise. "The weak can never forgive," insisted Mahatma Gandhi. "Forgiveness is the attribute of the strong."

Chapter 10

Kiss and Make Up?

In his native Sicily, Father Giuseppe Puglisi is revered as a hero. In fact, the formal process of his being declared a saint has begun, in light of his courageous ministry in an area plagued by the Mafia. He himself became a Mafia target and was gunned down by a hit man in 1993.

Father Puglisi's ministry began in a tiny village of just over 100 people. Because of Mafia violence, however, the village had witnessed fifteen murders. When he arrived in the village, Father Puglisi met this situation head-on. He went from door to door, speaking about forgiveness.

Thanks to his efforts, one woman felt compelled to forgive the mother of her son's assassin. In spite of great difficulties, Father Puglisi arranged for the two women to meet. Forgiveness was given and received, and the two women were reconciled, a beautiful occasion of healing amid a broken, divided, and violent community.[11]

True reconciliation can't happen without forgiveness, and God smiles when broken relationships are restored.

God himself became man in Jesus so we could be reconciled with him. In theology, this is called the "atonement." If that word is broken down into its parts, we have "at-one-ment." Thanks to what Jesus did, and the forgiveness he offers, we can be "at one" with God.

Forgiveness, however, doesn't always lead to reconciliation. Sometimes reconciliation just isn't possible. Perhaps the person we've forgiven has died, or maybe we'll never see him or her again, for whatever reason. Sometimes it's not advisable to reconcile with those we forgive. If they're dangerous, we would do well to avoid them. Jesus does call us to love our enemies, and that love includes forgiveness. However, when we see an enemy coming, or even just a person we find difficult, sometimes the best thing to do is to avoid that person. We can forgive from a distance those people we should keep at a distance.

At the same time, there are certain people in our lives with whom we should make every effort to reconcile, should there be a need to do so. They're part of what we might call our "primary relationships." Our forgiveness of them wouldn't be complete, or authentic, without an attempt at reconciliation. Jesus taught that if we're on our way to worship, and we have something against our "brother," we should first be reconciled with him before we approach the altar (Mt 5:23–4). When speaking of our "brother," Jesus means either a relative or a fellow Christian. We may understand him, however, as referring to all those in our primary relationships. They're the people who should be a part of our lives no matter what. Because of that, if we don't seek to reconcile with them, even if we think we've forgiven them, there will always be a distance between us, a disconnect, an awkwardness.

That's one reason why, after his Resurrection, Jesus reconciles with Peter (Jn 21:15–19). It happens early one morning by the Sea of Tiberias, where the disciples have been fishing all night in boats. When Peter sees Jesus at the water's edge, he dives into the water and swims to shore as fast as he can. He finds Jesus standing next to a charcoal fire. The last time Peter had been described as being next to a charcoal fire, he was in the courtyard of the house where Jesus was on trial. Just as Jesus had predicted, Peter denied knowing Jesus three times before a rooster crowed. On this morning, however, Peter does something else. In answer to his questions, three times Peter assures Jesus that he loves him. When they are through, a magnificent reconciliation has taken place.

Before this event, Peter knew that Jesus had risen from the dead. They'd seen each other, and surely they'd exchanged words. This must certainly have filled Peter with joy! At the same time, we can imagine the pain in his heart, the shame he felt whenever he saw the friend he'd abandoned. In the courtyard, after Peter's third denial, Jesus had looked Peter in the eye. Could Peter look Jesus in the eye now? Or would he instead turn away and stare at his feet whenever Jesus directed his gaze at him? Peter must have replayed in his mind, over and over again, the tears he wept after he heard the rooster crow. But after Jesus reaches out and reconciles with him, Peter's burden is lifted. Their relationship is restored.

Jesus calls us, whenever one of our primary relationships has been bruised or broken, to seek reconciliation, as he did with Peter. Certainly husbands and wives should do this, as God called them together to become "one flesh." So, too, parents and children—and that includes adult children. The Ten Commandments instruct children to honor their parents, and parents should likewise honor their children. The Bible insists that unity within the Church between fellow Christians is of paramount importance. In fact, the night before he died, Jesus prayed that all his followers might "be one," just as he and the Father "are one" (Jn 17:21).

When seeking to reconcile, we should never wait until it's too late. I knew a woman who refused to reconcile with her estranged son, even though she insisted she'd forgiven him. But she was still too angry and proud to reach out to him. Thankfully, on her deathbed, she and her son had a long talk, truly forgave each other, and embraced. She died with more peace than she'd had in years. But so many others with broken primary relationships fail to do this. Don't let yourself be filled with regret at a funeral parlor, apologizing to someone who can't respond.

Sure, there are risks in seeking to reconcile. In family feuds, for example, people sometimes take sides. If we try to heal the breach, some of our relatives may think we're a "sellout" or a traitor. They may say, "How can you even speak with him after what he's done to our family?" As the old saying goes, "No good deed goes unpunished." But if that's the case with us, we'll be in good company. Jesus was punished for his good deeds. But that's the price he was willing to pay to be reconciled with us.

CHAPTER 11

All Things Are Possible

During the Nazi occupation of Holland, Corrie ten Boom and her family were part of an underground network that hid Jewish families. Ultimately, the ten Booms were betrayed and imprisoned in dreadful concentration camps. Both Corrie's father and sister died while in prison.

Corrie had a deep and vibrant Christian faith. Nevertheless, it took her a long time to be freed of the hatred she felt for her persecutors. However, once she believed that she had forgiven them, she traveled the globe, sharing a message of love and forgiveness, seeking to heal the wounds that continued after the war.

One night in Munich, Corrie spoke to a German audience. A man approached her, held out his hand, and said, "How good it is to know that, as you say, all our sins are at the bottom of the sea!" Corrie was horrified to recognize him as one of the cruelest guards from her concentration camp. He had once forced her and others to

shower naked before him. She tried to shake his hand,
but her arm remained frozen at her side. The anger and
hatred she thought were behind her were still there.
"Jesus," she prayed in desperation, "help me." Just then
she was overcome by a feeling that she was loved and
forgiven. Her arm raised, and she clasped the hand of her
former enemy. Later she would write: "For a long moment
we grasped each other's hands, the former guard and the
former prisoner. I had never known God's love so
intensely as I did then."[12]

We can respond to amazing stories of forgiveness
such as this in one of two ways. On the one hand, we can
feel inspired and filled with hope—hope that we too can
forgive even the worst offenses. On the other hand, we
can feel discouraged, concluding that radical forgiveness
is possible only for truly exceptional, holy people, not
ordinary people like us. We fear that we could never find
it within ourselves to forgive an enemy who attacked us,
a friend who abandoned us, a spouse who betrayed us,
or someone who harmed one of our children. And our
fears would be justified. No matter how hard we try, we
can't find it within ourselves to forgive such people. It's
only from outside that we can find such strength.

Jesus is well aware of this. He does teach us to forgive, to be merciful, and to love our enemies. If he didn't
think we could do it, he wouldn't have said such things.
He'd never ask us to do the impossible. It is possible for
us to forgive, but only with his help. When it comes to
forgiveness, Jesus doesn't give us an "unfunded mandate," a costly law imposed without any help to carry it
out. He does give us a mandate to forgive. At the same
time, he gives us the grace we need to do it.

When it comes to forgiving a great hurt, it can seem as if we've been given an impossible mission. We may desperately want to forgive. Our intentions may be good, but we just can't follow through. It's as Jesus says to his sleepy disciples: "The spirit is willing, but the flesh is weak." So we find ourselves stuck. But that's not a bad place to be, because it can lead us to reach out to God and to say, "I just can't do this." Then God will say to us, "You're absolutely right. But I can. Allow me to help." And if we let him, he will.

Forgiveness is a decision. It requires an act of the will. Yet we can't rely on willpower alone. What we need is a higher power. In other words, to forgive like Jesus, we can't simply imitate Jesus. Instead, we need the help of Jesus himself. Only he can make possible what we thought was impossible. As St. Paul came to learn, "I can do all things through Christ, who strengthens me."

This lesson was also learned by a Catholic missionary, as told by Father John Monbourquette in *How to Forgive*. The missionary was unexpectedly removed from his ministry by his provincial superior. He became resentful, and he recognized a need to forgive. From then on the missionary had a new mission, a mission to forgive. With great determination he prayed and prayed for his provincial. Over and over again he said, "I forgive you" as he pictured his provincial in his mind. But nothing worked. His bitterness remained, and he became discouraged.

Not willing to give up, he made a retreat with the sole aim of achieving forgiveness. But after three days, he was still struggling and feeling hurt. Then he randomly picked up a Bible and the words "God alone can forgive" leaped off the page. He realized that he had been trying to forgive through his own efforts, an effort doomed to fail. He began to "let go and let God," as a popular phrase puts it, and was soon able to extend the forgiveness he was unable to give on his own.[13]

"To err is human . . . ," wrote Alexander Pope. And at one level, what he said is absolutely true. Every one of us, without exception, "errs." We hurt others; we hurt ourselves; we turn our backs on God. However, at another level, Pope's words need a qualification. We are made in God's image; we are created for holiness and perfection. To err, then, is to be less than human. It's a reflection of our weakened, fallen condition. This weakness also prevents us from forgiving like God. That's why we can't forgive without God. But Pope knew this, which is why he completed his famous quote the way he did: "To err is human; *to forgive, divine*."

PART III

HOW TO FORGIVE

CHAPTER 12

Pray It Through

A seminary classmate of mine was once a greengrocer in a small English village. If you wanted fresh fruits and vegetables, and you happened to live in that village, you had to visit *him*. The problem was, he was usually cranky and sometimes downright mean. One day, three of his regular customers, all older, retired women, decided to do something about his behavior. They didn't chew him out, and they didn't decide to go to the next village to buy their produce. Instead, they agreed that they would pray for him every day. And so they did.

Months passed, and one Sunday my classmate decided to take an early morning stroll. After a while he heard a church bell calling the faithful to worship. As a non-churchgoer, he ordinarily would have ignored the bells and kept on walking. This time, however, he felt something tugging at his heart, drawing him toward the sound. He walked to the church, paused for a moment, pushed open the door, and took a seat in a pew. Then, from behind him, he heard whispering voices: "It's him! It's him! He's finally come!" My classmate turned around and saw three smiling elderly ladies who visited his store each day. Their prayers had been answered.

As with my seminary classmate, God can change people through the prayers of others. Whenever we have someone to forgive, prayer should always be part of our effort. As Jesus taught, "Pray for anyone who mistreats you" (Mt 5:44, CEV). We can pray that they might change, for their conversion, and that they would become more loving and lovable. As a popular slogan puts it, "Prayer changes things!" However, we can't expect overnight results. Because people take time to change, we need to persevere in our prayer.

Consider the experience of St. Monica and St. Augustine, who were mother and son. As a young adult, Augustine abandoned his faith and began living a wayward life. At times he treated his mother poorly. But Monica never gave up on her son, and she prayed for him every day. Eighteen years later, what she prayed for came to pass. Augustine returned to his roots, was baptized, and dedicated his life to God's service. He eventually became a great bishop and preacher. Monica's perseverance had paid off.

Sadly, some people strongly resist change. They're too set in their ways, or they're stuck in anger or negativity. We can always pray for them to change, because no person is ever beyond hope. But we can pray for much more than that. We can pray that God will bless them and fill them with happiness and peace. We can also pray for their healing.

We can pray for ourselves, too. It's one thing to pray that another person might change, but maybe we need to change as well. As all of us are responsible for our *actions*, we are responsible also for our *reactions*. Perhaps we need to pray for wisdom and courage in dealing with a difficult person. We can ask God to help us be more patient and understanding. Maybe we need to pray for thicker skin, because we're allowing others to upset us more than they should. In addition, we can pray that we ourselves might be filled with peace and healing.

Above all, we can pray for the grace to forgive. One way we can do this is by using our imagination. Whenever we pray the words in the Our Father, "Forgive us our trespasses, as we forgive those who trespass against us," we can picture in our mind the person we're trying to forgive. It's a way of saying, "Lord, please help me forgive this person as you've forgiven me."

One thing we shouldn't do is pray that the person we need to forgive be punished or harmed. Sometimes it's tempting to want God to strike someone down with a lightning bolt. Indeed, this is exactly how Jesus's disciples feel when they aren't welcomed by the people in one town. They ask Jesus if they should "call down fire from heaven" upon them! But Jesus will have none of that (Lk 9:51–56).

In our anger at being hurt, we too may want to call down fire upon someone's head. If that's the case, we should be honest with God about our thoughts and feelings. God knows what's in our hearts anyway; we can't hide anything from him. However, God wants us to share our thoughts and feelings with him in prayer.

In my pastoral ministry, people will often admit feeling frustrated, angry, and resentful. I'll say: "Thank you for sharing these things with me. But have you shared them with God?" Usually, the answer is no. Sometimes they're too afraid. They fear that if they tell God they wish someone would be zapped with a lightning bolt, they'll be zapped themselves! At other times, it's never occurred to them to express their thoughts and feelings to God. They were never taught to pray that way. So they only tell God those things they think he wants to hear.

But God doesn't want censored prayers. He wants honest prayers. Consider the "prayer book" of the Bible: the Psalms. A great number of the psalms are laments or complaints. They're a model for our prayers. It's perfectly acceptable to say to God: "How could you let this happen? It's not fair! I don't deserve this! You could fix all this right now; why don't you?" Maybe we hesitate to express ourselves this way, because at some level we know that our words reflect a lack of trust, overwhelming anger, or personal immaturity. That may very well be the case. But that's where we are, and that's where God meets us. When we let God meet us, we invite him to heal and help us.

When praying after being hurt, we can find inspiration from Mary, our Mother. We killed her Son! As St. Francis of Assisi said, "It is [we] who have crucified him and crucify him still, when [we] delight in our vices and our sins." But what is Mary's response to this? Not rejection; not hatred. Instead, she accepts us as her children. And she prays for us, so that we might be able to pray—and forgive—as she did.

CHAPTER 13

Receive God's Forgiveness

St. Thérèse of Lisieux, the "Little Flower," told a story about a father who went to punish his two misbehaving sons. The first son, aware that he'd done wrong, ran away in fear. The other son, however, threw himself into his father's arms. He apologized for his behavior, made a promise to do better, told his father that he loved him, and asked to be "punished" with nothing more than a kiss. For his part, the father was more than happy to grant his son's wish.

Both boys, St. Thérèse explained, were sorry for what they'd done. The first was convinced that he'd have to face his father's wrath. The other son knew better. He asked for forgiveness, and a beautiful reconciliation took place. St. Thérèse stressed that the father knew full well that his son would misbehave again. Nevertheless, he was happy to forgive and "punish" with a kiss.

St. Thérèse's story is a parable of how our heavenly Father treats us. Our Father is merciful beyond description. There is nothing and no one he won't forgive; there's no such thing as a hopeless sinner. However, we sometimes hesitate to believe this. It seems just too good to be true. We may recite the Creed at Mass on Sundays and profess belief in "the forgiveness of sins," but it's as if we have our fingers crossed behind our backs. We doubt we'll be forgiven, and assume we'll be condemned instead.

These doubts and assumptions are challenged by a Scripture story in which a group of angry men confront Jesus with a woman they caught in the act of adultery (cf. Jn 8:1–11). She's presented as nameless and faceless, and we can only speculate about the circumstances that led to her predicament. All we're told is that she stood face to face with Jesus, guilty of a "sin of the flesh." Her fate rests in his hands, and she is certainly filled with terror, thinking that Jesus, like the men who encircled her, wants her stoned to death. How grateful and dumbstruck she must be when Jesus receives her with gentleness and mercy, and sends her away with nothing more than an instruction not to sin again.

In a similar fashion, many of us, conscious of sin, find ourselves terrified at the prospect of standing face to face with Jesus. Like the woman in the Scripture story, we confuse Jesus with the stone throwers. So we go to great lengths to avoid him, and we run away if we think he's getting too close. We don't go to Confession, stop receiving Holy Communion, and may even abandon church altogether. Surely, we're tempted to think, our sins must have crossed a line that Jesus has drawn in the sand somewhere. We know from our own experience how hard it can be to forgive other people, and we conclude that Jesus must have a hard time forgiving us as well.

But Jesus wants to forgive us, and it's not hard for him to do at all. He tells us so. As he is teaching in a house, a paralyzed man on a stretcher is brought to the house by four friends, in the hope that Jesus would heal him. The house is so crowded, however, that the man has to be lowered through the roof. When Jesus sees this, he forgives the man's sins before he's even had a chance to speak. The crowd is astonished, even scandalized. Jesus sees the crowd's reaction and says: "Which is easier, to say, 'Your sins are forgiven,' or to say, 'Rise and walk?' " Jesus does heal the paralyzed man, but not until he has made it quite clear to everyone there that he finds it easy to forgive. The man he heals is no longer confined to his stretcher. Most importantly, however, he is no longer bound by his sins (see Lk 5:17–26).

As he did with that man, Jesus wants to release us from our sins. If we don't let him, we'll wind up paralyzed. Not physically paralyzed, like the man Jesus healed, but spiritually paralyzed by guilt. Scripture describes how we can feel when we don't bring our sins to God for forgiveness: "When I declared not my sin, my body wasted away, / through my groaning all day long. / For day and night your hand was heavy upon me; / my strength was dried up as by the heat of summer" (Ps 32:3–4, RSV). When the psalmist finally brought his sins to God, however, he was filled with peace and joy.

Guilt isn't necessarily a bad thing. The feeling of guilt shows that we have a conscience and that we understand that our actions can hurt others. Only sociopaths feel no guilt! But guilt does not have to paralyze us. Instead, it can provide the energy that spurs us into action, leading us to seek forgiveness from God, that our relationship with him might be restored.

It's terribly hard to forgive when we're paralyzed by guilt. It's much easier to do what's right when our relationship with God is right and our conscience is at peace. Simply put, people who know they're forgiven are much more likely to be people who forgive. We can forgive like God only if we know we've been forgiven by God. How could we deny to others what has so generously been given to us? Therefore, when faced with the need to forgive another, we need to seek the forgiveness of God: in heartfelt prayer, at the altar, in the confessional.

Jesus taught that those who are forgiven much, love much (see Lk 7:47). We can be grateful that we have a God who loves to forgive. It's true to say that God wants to forgive us more than we could ever want to sin. That's why he entered our world, in Jesus his Son. Jesus didn't come to condemn the world; he came to save it, and he longs to forgive us. We might even say that he's dying to forgive us—which is exactly what he has already done!

CHAPTER 14

"Bless Me, Father . . ."

Steven McDonald was one of New York's finest, a young police officer from a family of police officers. Only twenty-nine years old, he was a newlywed, and his wife was expecting their first child, a boy. But one summer afternoon in 1986, Steven found himself in Central Park confronting a teenager named Shavod Jones. The youth pulled a gun and fired three times, hitting Steven in the head and neck. While Steven lay bleeding on the ground, pleading with God for his life, Shavod ran off. Steven survived but was permanently paralyzed from the neck down. He spent the next eighteen months in a hospital.

Before this tragedy, Steven had not been especially committed to his Catholic faith, but being shot changed everything. He reached out to God for help, as did his wife, Patti Ann. God reached right back to them, inspiring Steven to forgive the young man who had so dramatically changed his life. The following year, in the hospital chapel where Steven's son had just been baptized, Patti Ann read a statement on Steven's behalf. It concerned Shavod Jones. "I forgive him," wrote Steven, "and hope that he can find peace and purpose in his life."[14]

After his release from the hospital, Steven began a public speaking campaign. Using a wheelchair controlled by puffs of his breath, and talking with difficulty because of his ventilator, Steven touched countless lives with his message of nonviolence and forgiveness. He said, "I would often tell people that the only thing worse than a bullet in my spine would have been to nurture revenge in my heart." He explained the importance of his Catholic faith in helping him to forgive Shavod Jones. In particular, he spoke of the necessity of regular Confession in helping him to become a forgiving person. "Seeking God's forgiveness," he insisted, "implies forgiving others."[15]

Steven McDonald will never be completely healed from his terrible gunshot wounds. He has, however, experienced tremendous healing in his soul through Confession. It's for good reason that Confession (known also as Reconciliation or Penance) has traditionally been classified as a sacrament of healing. Sin needs healing. Sin wounds us, it wounds others, and it strains our relationship with God. But in Confession, our sins are forgiven, we receive healing for sin's wounds, and we're strengthened to forgive the sins of others.

I've witnessed the healing effects of this sacrament with those adults who make their first Confession prior to being received into the Church. Beforehand, they're often anxious, embarrassed, and even afraid, but when they're done, they're walking on cloud nine. They feel as if a great weight has been lifted off their shoulders, and their faces shine with joy. By confessing, they give God an opportunity to show them how much he loves and cares for them, and this experience fills them with peace.

We cheat ourselves of this peace when we fail to confess our sins. Not confessing our sins only adds to the wounds they caused in the first place. Keeping our sins bottled up within us never does any good. They fester inside us and eat away at our souls. Trying to keep something from God creates a big block in our relationship with him. We may try to pray, but if we have unconfessed sins, they become the proverbial elephant in the room. It's not as if we can keep secrets from God. He knows our every thought and feeling and sees within the depths of our souls. Ordinarily this should fill us with consolation and joy! But when we have unconfessed sins, we'll feel awkward at best, or full of dread at worst. When we feel this way, we'll find it difficult to forgive. Since we feel condemned ourselves, we'll likely condemn others.

But maybe our conscience isn't troubling us too much. We don't see a need for Confession. We say to ourselves, "I'm basically a good person. I don't do anything *that* wrong. So why should I bother?" We conclude that if we're decent, well-intentioned, fundamentally responsible human beings, there's no real need to go to Confession. With this understanding, Confession isn't for those who are "basically good." It's only for those who are "basically bad." The reality is, however, that Jesus hasn't called us to be good people. He calls us to be holy people, and holiness involves a serious struggle with sin. If we can't see sin when we look at our lives, we're not necessarily holy. We're probably just blind.

Sometimes we're aware of our sins, but we've become too comfortable with them. Things we used to wince at are now things we wink at. We shrug our shoulders and say, "That's just the way I am," or we blame our surroundings. We can convince ourselves that our sins are excused by all the good we do; we think of them like "time off for good behavior." We can get to the point where we don't want to change our ways or don't think we have to. Our hearts become indifferent. Sometimes, our hearts will become hard. As Pope John Paul II said, "When we forget we are sinners, we forget our need for Christ. And when we forget we need Christ, we have lost everything!"

People who see no need to be forgiven typically see no need to forgive. People who deny themselves God's forgiveness typically deny forgiveness to other people. If we fit either of these descriptions, Jesus invites us to reconsider the role of Confession in our faith life. He asks us to put aside our fear and indifference, and to open our hearts to him in that healing sacrament: so we can know the joy of his forgiveness; so others can know the joy of being forgiven by us. "Christians need to learn to forgive," explained Mother Teresa. "How do we learn to forgive? By knowing that we, too, need to be forgiven."

Chapter 15

Broken Bread
for Broken People

Early one weekday morning while celebrating Mass, I looked out at the congregation and, as usual, recognized many of those present. They were the regulars, you might say. As I scanned the faces in the pews, I recalled their personal situations, as they had shared them with me. There were those struggling with various health issues and addictions. Some were agonizing with divorce, others were estranged from adult children. A few were having a challenging time caring for family members who were aging, sick, or unable to live independently. One woman longed to be a mother but kept failing to conceive, while another, a mother of many children, was at her wits' end. There was a lonely widower, a lonely young transplant from another city, and a lonely immigrant from a distant country. There were those stuck in painful relationships and others trapped in painful work environments. In fact, there was some measure of pain in the life of just about everyone there. I then thought about the struggles and pains in my own life, and it dawned on me that all of us at that Mass were gathered around the altar in our brokenness, having come to Jesus in hope that he might put the broken pieces back together and make us whole again.

Every time you and I come to Mass, we bring with us our particular burdens, struggles, and heartaches. Perhaps we're stressed by life's demands, concerned about our relationships, under pressure to make ends meet, worried about our kids, or grieving the loss of a loved one. We may face poor health, loneliness, or frustrations at work. We regret past choices, carry baggage from our past, and wrestle with bad habits. We've hurt others, others have hurt us, and we've hurt ourselves. We come to Jesus around his altar in our brokenness, and at that altar we're reminded that Jesus himself knew brokenness. He was physically broken with nails, whips, fists, thorns, and a spear. He knew the brokenness of being abandoned and even betrayed by friends. He was mocked, insulted, and cursed. His fellow countrymen, the religious leadership, and the government all rejected him. He was a victim of bigotry by those who mistrusted or hated Galileans or Jews. He was a victim of the cowardice of those who arrested and condemned him under the cover of darkness. And while Jesus himself never committed a sin, he took the burden of our sins upon himself and knew the agonizing separation from God they cause us when he cried, "My God, my God, why have you forsaken me?" (Mk 15:34).

In his love for us, Jesus allowed himself to be broken in many ways. We're reminded of this at Mass when the priest takes the consecrated host, the bread that's become the Body of Christ, and breaks it while the congregation prays, "Lamb of God, you take away the sins of the world." One reason the host is broken is to remind us that Jesus was broken.

However, after the host is broken, the priest takes a small piece of the host and drops it into the chalice containing the wine that has become the Blood of Christ. This signifies that while Jesus's body and blood were separated at the crucifixion, they were reunited at the Resurrection. In other words, at Mass we come before the once-broken Jesus who has been made whole again. Then this Jesus meets us in our brokenness, and he seeks to make us whole as well.

To do this, he gives us himself, his *eu charis*, Greek for "good gift," and heals us. He gives us the grace to carry on in patient endurance. He fills us with the consolation of the Holy Spirit. He provides us with the wisdom to see our difficulties in the way that he sees them. He showers us with gifts of faith, hope, and love. He comes to us in person to take away our loneliness. He forgives us those everyday sins through which we wound others and wound ourselves, and he gives us the strength to forgive those who've wounded us.

St. Thomas Aquinas wrote about the Eucharist: "Among the sacraments, no other has greater power to heal. Through it, sins are removed, virtues increased, and the soul enriched with every spiritual gift in abundance." That's why, when we're faced with the necessity of forgiving, especially when we find forgiving to be hard, we should come to Mass as often as possible.

When we've been hurt by another, we've been broken in some way. We may have a broken heart or a broken spirit. Even our body may have been broken or wounded. In our brokenness, we can go to Jesus at Mass and pray, "Lord, I am not worthy that you should enter under my roof, but only say the word and my soul shall be healed." Then we receive Jesus, and he fills us with healing grace. Through the forgiveness of our sins, we're healed of the wounds we inflict on ourselves. We're healed of the brokenness we've received at the hands of others, by being strengthened and consoled. We're then sent forth into the world to share that forgiveness and healing with others.

We're not sent forth alone, however. Jesus comes with us. In a very real way, he is our companion. "Companion" is derived from two Latin words: *cum*, which means "with"; and *pane*, the word for "bread." When we set forth to forgive, then, it is Jesus himself who is our bread for the journey; he gives us the nourishment to do what we need to do.

Before Mass, that nourishment began as ordinary bread. When it was brought forward by the congregation to the altar, that bread represented an offering to Jesus of our very lives and livelihood, including our brokenness. That bread was then blessed and broken by a priest's hands. But now it's no longer just bread. It's the Bread of Life. It's Jesus. He who was broken for us gives us broken bread that we might be made whole, as he was made whole. And then we go forth together, to share that gift with the world. Through love. Through compassion. Through mercy. Through forgiveness.

CHAPTER 16

Forgive Yourself

As happens with so many young adults, a seventeenth-century Portuguese shepherd and soldier drifted away from his faith. One day, however, during a big religious festival, he heard a powerful homily preached by Blessed John of Avila. Right in the middle of the crowd, the young man began to cry out loud, beat his breast, and scream for mercy at the top of his lungs. He continued this behavior for months. He became a public nuisance, wandering the streets and pleading for forgiveness. The locals concluded that he was insane and had him shut up in a local asylum.

John of Avila learned of this and paid him a visit. He convinced the young man that he'd punished himself long enough. It was time for him to spend his energies on something positive that would benefit both himself and his neighbors. The young man took this advice, and he dedicated the rest of his life to serving the sick and the poor.[16] We know him today as St. John of God.

When he first heard John of Avila's preaching, John of God knew that he needed to repent, to turn his life around. Unfortunately, how he went about it was too extreme. What, then, should repentance involve in practice? A crowd once asked that very question of John the Baptist (see Lk 3:10–14). "What then should we do?" they cried. In his reply, John the Baptist spoke of acting with generosity, honesty, simplicity, and fairness. He did not say, "Beat yourself up." We can and should lament our sins and the damage they do, but, at the same time, we should always rejoice in our redemption. We might hate some of the things we've done, but we should never hate ourselves. God doesn't.

True repentance involves positive change, not being consumed with regret. It involves turning away from sin with trust and hope in God's mercy and forgiveness. Repentance also requires that we forgive ourselves, as God forgives us. As C. S. Lewis once wrote, "If God forgives us, we must forgive ourselves. Otherwise it is almost like setting ourselves up as a higher tribunal than God."

Sometimes, however, good people fail to forgive themselves for bad things they've done. In the confessional, they'll confess things they admit they've confessed before, sometimes over and over again. It's obvious that what they've done is still troubling them. I'll ask if they believe that Jesus has forgiven them. Usually they'll answer yes. Then I'll ask, "But have you forgiven yourself?" Almost always the answer is no.

By not forgiving ourselves, we become consumed by shame and guilt, and we are burdened with regrets over past choices. We'll say things like, "If only I'd done this" or "If only I hadn't done that." Perhaps we've engaged in self-destructive behavior like heavy drinking or compulsive gambling. Maybe we made poor choices when raising our children or caring for elderly parents. It could be that we're tortured over past sexual indiscretions or an abortion. Possibly we made poor financial or career choices, rushed into an ill-advised relationship, or contributed to a relationship's failure. Or it could be that we didn't do something we should have, such as intervening in a family crisis or stopping a friend from driving drunk. If we don't forgive ourselves for such things, we'll find it terribly hard to forgive anyone else. We can't give what we don't have.

Failure to forgive ourselves is a self-inflicted wound. It's normal to feel bad when we've hurt others or hurt ourselves, but feeling bad is different from self-pity. When we fail to forgive ourselves, we wind up feeling sorry for ourselves. Then we'll want others to feel sorry for us too, because we're so miserable. At every turn we find ourselves sending out invitations to our own pity party. For consolation, we might turn to alcohol, drugs, or food. Or, like John of God, we turn on ourselves, imposing unnecessary penances.

God doesn't want us doing unnecessary penances. There are, however, appropriate penances he's happy for us to do, things that add love and goodness to a world we've darkened through our sins. For instance, if we've hurt another person, we can apologize to him or her. Even if that person doesn't accept our apology, we've at least taken responsibility for our actions. We can also try to make amends for the things we've done. Perhaps we can do something kind for the person we've hurt, or, if that isn't possible, we can do something kind for someone else. The best way to feel good is to do good. That's what John of Avila counseled John of God to do. It worked, and John of God was transformed from desperation into sainthood.

Doing good can help us forgive ourselves. There are other things we can do, too. The consolation of God's love we receive by making a good confession is important. We can also change the way we think. Instead of thinking over and over again about our past wrong, we should concentrate instead about God's mercy, or recall kind deeds we've performed. This isn't a denial of what we've done wrong, but a realization that being obsessed with our misdeeds helps no one—including ourselves. It's also important to pray, asking God for the grace to forgive ourselves and learn from our mistakes instead of being crushed by them.

God is always trying to make us into better people by correcting us, challenging us, encouraging us, and sending special people and opportunities into our lives. To teach us trust, humility, and compassion, he may allow us to suffer. To make us responsible, he allows us to face the consequences of our actions. He doesn't impose the consequences; they spring from our choices. In other words, when we sin, God doesn't turn his back on us; it's we who turn our backs on him. Sin is its own punishment. That's why Mother Teresa could insist, "God does not punish." So why do we punish ourselves? Let's forgive ourselves instead. Then, let's forgive others.

CHAPTER 17

Walk in Their Shoes

E benezer Scrooge, Charles Dickens's character from *A Christmas Carol*, was heartless, miserly, and cruel for most of his adult life. But during his visit from the Ghost of Christmas Past, we're given a glimpse into the difficult childhood he endured. His father cared little for him, and he was left to spend the Christmas holidays alone at his stern boarding school. Dickens suggests that having been unloved as a child contributed to Scrooge becoming so unloving later in life.

A difficult childhood didn't excuse Scrooge from his behavior as an adult. He was accountable for the person he'd allowed himself to become. That's why he needed visits from the three ghosts! But understanding that Scrooge's childhood was unhappy allows us to appreciate the circumstances that gave rise to his behavior.

Understanding a person's difficult circumstances can help us to have empathy for them and to forgive them. Appreciating that they may have been hurt can help us pardon them when they hurt us. As Henry Wadsworth Longfellow wrote, "If we could read the secret history of our enemies, we should find in each man's life sorrow and suffering enough to disarm all hostility" (*Drift-Wood*, 1857). The more we know, the easier it is to forgive.

People's negative behavior often arises from pain, fear, or ignorance, and is frequently an inappropriate attempt to meet a legitimate need. Bullies, for instance, are sometimes victims of bullying themselves. Their efforts to intimidate or humiliate others are an attempt to conceal shame or anxiety or boost a very low self-esteem. Husbands and wives may be tempted to cheat because they feel unloved or unconnected. Catholic spiritual writer Henri Nouwen found himself humbled by prison inmates to whom he ministered when he realized that their crimes were a cry for help. "Many of these brothers and sisters," he observed, "have never known or felt the safe touch of a loving hand."[17]

Sometimes there's a medical or physical reason behind problem behavior. Illness, depression, and fatigue can make people angry and irritable. Teenagers do reckless things because the part of their brain that restrains risky activity isn't fully developed yet. Adults with ADHD may appear to their partners to be thoughtless, selfish, and uncaring toward them or their family. But these are symptoms of a disorder, not intentional neglect.

As with Ebenezer Scrooge, the environment in which individuals are raised can greatly influence how they live life as an adult. This was one conclusion of a study of pre-World War II German society, sponsored by the state of Israel to help understand the causes of the Holocaust. It was determined that those German children who had been taught to give blind obedience to authority under the threat of physical punishment had been primed to submit, as adults, to the oppressive authority of the Nazi party. Their upbringing later became a moral handicap.[18]

But regardless of whether a person has acted out of fear, ignorance, illness, or deep pain, when they've hurt us, we're tempted to demonize them. In other words, we see them as all bad. Seeing someone this way is like the opposite of being in love. When we've fallen in love, the object of our affection can do no wrong. In our infatuation, we overlook or ignore faults. When we've been deeply hurt, however, we tend to see the other person as nothing more than the source of our grief. While in love, we see others through rose-colored glasses; while in pain, we view them through crosshairs.

It's terribly difficult to forgive someone we've demonized. In Jesus's day, whole categories of people were demonized by being publicly labeled as sinners. They were to be shamed and scorned, not forgiven. Some thought it better to spit in their faces than greet them in the street; some might have considered it better to kill one's daughter rather than allow her to marry such a person. Jesus, however, welcomed the scorned, taught them, ate with them, loved them. He didn't condemn them as sinners. Instead, we might say that he understood them as "people who sin." That's a big distinction. St. Augustine put it well: "Man and sinner are two different things. God made man, but man himself made the sinner."

When Jesus looks at someone, he doesn't just see their sins. He sees a person made in God's image; in that person's eyes he can see a little reflection of himself. That reflection is clearer in some than it is in others, to be sure! But in every person, without exception, Jesus sees someone worth redeeming, saving, forgiving.

When we see others as Jesus sees them, we'll be better able to forgive them as Jesus forgives them. Jesus knows full well that sometimes a person's bad behavior is a reflection of bad circumstances. In his love and mercy, he always takes that into account. St. Dorotheos of Gaza, a sixth-century monk of the Egyptian desert, shares a story contrasting the lives of two girls brought up in radically different ways. One was raised by a devout woman to live a good and holy life. The other lived with an exotic dancer by whom she "was trained in the works of the devil." St. Dorotheos explains that God expected much less of the girl raised in an immoral atmosphere. He asks, "Is it possible to say that what God asks from the one he also asks from the other? Surely not! How can he allow them to be examined by the same standard?"[19]

Jesus knew that those who crucified him didn't entirely understand what they were doing. That's often the case with those who hurt us: they act not from pure malice, but out of ignorance, pain, or fear. Their actions may be wrong, but their circumstances make them less responsible. It also makes it easier for us to forgive them. That's why Jesus invites us to make our own the words he cried from the cross: "Father, forgive them, they know not what they do" (Lk 23:34).

CHAPTER 18

Lower the Bar

A lot of contemporary pop singers express a hope that someone will "save" them: save them from loneliness, save them from despair, save them from the person they've allowed themselves to become. They express a heartfelt and sometimes desperate longing to be happy, wanted, and fulfilled.

If it's true that art imitates life, many people today are looking and longing for someone to save them. And that shouldn't surprise us, for we all need saving! The good news of Christianity is that we can be saved by another person, but not by just any person. Not a lover, a politician, or a guru—the only one who can truly save us is Jesus, God-become-man.

When we look to any other person to save us, we expect them to fulfill a need that only Jesus can fulfill. That's a heavy burden to place upon anyone and guarantees the person will ultimately fail. Because there's no way he or she will live up to our expectations, we'll inevitably feel let down. We'll wind up angry, frustrated, and disappointed, but that's our fault, because we were being unrealistic.

Other people can indeed provide us a strong dose of happiness and joy. They can relieve a measure of our loneliness. Our relationships with them can help give our lives direction and purpose, but they can't fulfill our ultimate needs. Only Jesus can do that. Other people are just as weak, broken, and finite as we are. To some degree, they will always disappoint us. I was once given a very meaningful penance in Confession, and it's something I still do to this day: Every time I pass before the Blessed Sacrament, I genuflect and pray, "Lord, only you can satisfy my deepest longing for love." It's good to be reminded of that often.

We need to have realistic expectations of others, just as Jesus has realistic expectations of us. He doesn't expect us to do what we're incapable of doing, and he certainly doesn't expect us to be flawless. Consider Jesus's disciples. Jesus knew full well what he was getting when he called them to ministry. At times, they were a less-than-impressive group. They frustrated Jesus because they didn't "get it." They were sleepy cowards the night Jesus was arrested. James and John were vengeful and proud; Thomas had his doubts; Judas was a greedy betrayer. Finally, there was their leader, Peter. Hot-tempered and boastful, he denied even knowing Jesus.

Jesus appreciated that his disciples were a work in progress. We see this when Peter encounters Jesus after the Resurrection (see Jn 21:15–19). At first, Jesus asks Peter twice, "Do you love me?" In the original New Testament Greek, the word translated as "love" is *agape*—the sacrificial, self-giving type of love that Jesus showed on the cross. In response, Peter affirms that he loves Jesus, but the love Peter refers to is not *agape* but *phileo*, the love of friendship and brotherhood. It's as if Peter had said, "Lord, you know I'm your friend."

Why did Peter say this? Just days earlier, Peter boasted that he was ready to die for Jesus! Yet within hours, Peter, in his weakness and fear, completely disowned Jesus. That's why he didn't say he loved Jesus the way Jesus asked him to love him. He was just being honest. Jesus understood. When he asked Peter a third time for an assurance of his love, Jesus no longer used the word *agape*. He used *phileo* instead. It's as if Jesus had asked him, "Peter, are you my friend?" To which Peter readily agreed. He knew that he wasn't yet capable of *agape* love, and Jesus knew it too. That's why he didn't demand of Peter what Peter was incapable of giving.[20]

Jesus had realistic expectations for his disciples. He's realistic with us, too. He knows that we're far from perfect. After all, even the saints weren't perfect, this side of heaven. The criterion for sainthood is not perfection, but "heroic virtue"—a big difference. Jesus doesn't demand perfection. The problem is sometimes we do. Perfectionists are hard on others, and they're hard on themselves. Their expectations are just too high; perfectionism only leaves room for failure. That's why perfectionists typically wind up frustrated, and those around them end up hurt.

If we tend to be perfectionists, we need to be aware of this. Even if we aren't perfectionists, at some point most of us will place unrealistic expectations upon others. A newlywed may expect his partner to change into the person he wants her to be. Parents expect children to follow in their footsteps or fulfill the dreams they impose on them instead of letting them chart their own course. We can even attach expectations to our forgiveness. We expect those we've forgiven to change their ways, express gratitude for our pardon, or at the very least start being nice to us.

Sometimes our expectations are a reflection of our neediness or our pain. For instance, when her husband became bedridden after a tragic accident, one distressed woman demanded unreasonable amounts of attention and assistance from those who weren't able to give it. She drove them away and deprived herself of the help and care they were prepared to give. In the process, she became a deeply bitter, angry person.

By feeling disappointed when others fail to meet our unrealistic expectations, we may conclude that we need to forgive them even though they haven't done anything that needs forgiving! We're the ones who created the problem, not them. The solution? Lower the bar. We can't expect others to give more than they're capable of giving; we can't expect others to be who they aren't; and we certainly can't expect them to be perfect.

Yes, Jesus did tell us to "be perfect, just as your heavenly Father is perfect" (Mt 5:48), but he didn't mean that we need to be flawless. If that were the case, we'd have to admit we're in bad shape! What he did mean is that we need to love as God the Father loves: without condition. Such love requires that we *accept* not *expect*. If we can learn to love like that, we'll realize that there is much less to forgive than we may once have thought.

CHAPTER 19

What Did I Do?

In a magazine interview, Paul McCartney was reminded that his song "Yesterday," which he wrote as a Beatle, has been covered—or redone by other artists and bands—more than 3,000 times. Paul admitted that he finds it funny how his lyrics have been changed in many of those versions. The original words are: "I said something wrong, now I long for yesterday." The singer admits his wrongdoing and understands why a woman he loved has left him. In the cover versions (he mentioned Elvis by name) this line gets altered to: "I *must've* said something wrong." Paul interprets this change to mean: "I doubt very much if I did." The implication of this is that the singer was innocent, and the woman who left him was mistaken or too sensitive. The breakup was her fault, not his.[21]

That "Yesterday" has been changed in this way time and again is an indication of how hard it is to admit our wrongdoings and accept responsibility for our actions.

It's much easier to make excuses, point the finger at someone else, or hide behind the circumstances in which we find ourselves. When we do this, we're like a child who accidentally breaks Mama's favorite vase, but, instead of owning up to it, accuses the dog.

When considering a situation in which we've been hurt, it's easy to place all the blame on the one who offended us. It's possible, however, that we had a role to play as well. We might share some of the blame for the circumstances that led up to our hurt. This doesn't excuse the other person entirely. Others are responsible for their actions, but isn't it possible that those actions could be a reaction to something we might have done? Did their hurting us have anything to do with our having hurt them in some way? Those are questions we might consider when we're trying to forgive. It's easier to forgive another when we accept that we might need forgiveness from them.

In his preaching, Jesus asks a question for which he didn't provide an answer. Perhaps he did this because he wants us to answer this question for ourselves; maybe he did this because the answer will be a little bit different for each one of us. The question is: Why do we notice other people's faults but ignore ours? Or to quote Jesus exactly, "Why do you notice the splinter in your brother's eye, but do not perceive the wooden beam in your own?" (Lk 6:41).

There are many reasons why we might do this. Maybe we're too afraid or ashamed to admit our faults. Perhaps focusing on others' faults makes us feel better about our own. It's possible that we're ignoring our faults because we don't want to deal with them. Or it could be that we don't even realize that they're there in the first place; we may need another person to help us identify what they are. Also, when we've been deeply hurt through the faults of others, our pain can blind us from seeing that our faults may have hurt them too.

Simple laziness can lead us to dismiss our faults, because it's just easier to blame somebody else for our troubles than to accept responsibility for them ourselves. So we complain: "It's my job that's driving me to drink!" or "My parents made me the way I am!" or "I'm not cheating on my taxes; the government's stealing *my* money," or "You'd do it too if you were married to him/her!" Then there's the classic: "The devil made me do it." Sometimes we make lame excuses for our faults. We say things like: "Everybody does it," or "I'm not really hurting anyone," or "I'm too set in my ways to change," or "God has bigger things to worry about," or "C'mon! This was the only fun I had all week!"

Another reason why we notice others' faults and ignore our own is because we tend to evaluate other people based on their *behavior*, while we evaluate ourselves based on our *intentions*. For instance, when we're speeding it's because we're in a hurry for a very important reason. On the other hand, when we see others speeding, we label them reckless drivers. While we're quick to condemn others, we're just as quick to excuse ourselves, even if we've done exactly the same thing. We rationalize that we act upon the best of motives, while we assume that others do not.

To admit our faults is to acknowledge our weakness. Unfortunately, our culture prizes power, domination, control, and aggressive independence, while weaknesses are dismissed as liabilities. "Weakness is defeat!" is a popular motivational slogan in the military. Maybe there's truth in that on a battlefield. But in the battle of the spiritual life, admitting weakness is something of a victory. It shows that we're in touch with reality. It can help us appreciate the weaknesses of others, and it can help us forgive.

We need the humility, courage, and self-love necessary to honestly examine ourselves, to accept our weaknesses, and to admit our faults. Only then will we be able to examine others' lives and actions with clear vision and a clean conscience. We'll recognize that there are always two sides to every story. We'll be able to see a situation better from another's point of view, and we'll be able to accept any role we may have played in those times we've been hurt. Did we not leave when we should have? Did we talk when we should have kept silent? Were we arrogant? Rude? Insensitive? Thoughtless? Selfish? Or did we simply not care or pay attention?

A person who has hurt us may insist: "You were asking for it!" That's not true; our behavior didn't give another person the license to hurt us. However, to appreciate that someone may think that way can make it easier to give the gift of forgiveness. The person may not be "asking for it." But God most certainly is.

CHAPTER 20

Get Mad,
Just Don't Get Even

The Temple in Jerusalem is packed. The faithful have come from far and wide to celebrate Passover. Jesus himself is there to do the very same thing and to teach the people. But what he sees happening to those people disturbs him. Moneychangers are charging them outrageously high rates so they can pay the annual Temple tax with coins that don't bear pagan images. To make their expected religious sacrifices, the pilgrims are essentially forced to purchase grossly overpriced animals from vendors within the Temple precincts. Reasonably priced animals are available in the city. Funny thing, though: only those animals bought from the Temple vendors ever seem to pass inspection by the Temple authorities. It's a corrupt system, and those responsible for it are lining their pockets at the expense of the poor.[22]

Jesus is furious at this injustice. While astonished crowds look on, he accuses those responsible of making God's house a "den of robbers," turns over their tables and chairs, and drives them out with a whip made of cords (see Mk 11:15–19). The Cleansing of the Temple, as this episode is traditionally called, makes it very clear that anger was not an emotion forbidden to Jesus.

Many Christians, however, think that anger is an emotion forbidden to them. They recall that Jesus commanded us to love our enemies and turn the other cheek. They conclude, therefore, that anger and Christian faith are incompatible. At best, they think, anger is a lamentable loss of self-control and at worst it's a grave sin.

Yet Jesus's anger can't be a sin, because Jesus never committed a sin. What's more, as Jesus lived the perfect human life, his every action has implications for our own behavior. We are to live in imitation of Christ, and the Christ we are to imitate was, at times, angry.

As with everything he did, the way Jesus expressed his anger was a reflection of his love. Think of it this way: if Jesus didn't care about God's Temple being turned into a "den of robbers," and if he didn't care for the welfare of the poor people who were being exploited, he could have turned a blind eye or shrugged his shoulders and walked away.

Jesus shows us that anger is our capacity to get "worked up" against injustice. It gives us the energy to confront that which is wrong, so that we might do something about it. St. Augustine described anger, along with its sister virtue courage, as daughters of hope. We can use our anger at the way things are to help change things into what they should be. To do that is an act of love.

Sometimes, however, anger doesn't express love. It may harden into resentment or self-pity, creating in us a thirst for retaliation. It may even erupt into blind rage. Because this may happen, we conclude that anger itself is the problem. But anger is simply a feeling, neither good nor bad. It's how we respond to our feelings of anger that is either right or wrong. When we've been hurt by another, we will typically feel angry. That's normal; it's okay. What matters most is how we process that anger. We need to avoid either trying to deny our anger or allowing ourselves to get stuck in it.

Anger can't be denied or repressed; it's an emotion that refuses to be ignored. Our feelings are an important part of us; if we deny them, we deny a part of ourselves. If we try to deny it, anger will fester deep within our souls, leaving us joyless, cynical, and depressed. Or it may surface in inappropriate reactions or be directed at undeserving people. For instance, we may have been hurt by our boss at work, but we end up yelling at our spouse or kicking the dog.

It's also possible to get stuck in our anger. We become deeply resentful; we want revenge against the one who has hurt us. At the very least, we slander the person who has hurt us far and wide, seeking to destroy his or her reputation. Our anger may become so intense that it boils over and explodes. Good judgment and reason fly out the window, and we do things we'll probably later regret. Anger does need to be released, but this is best done slowly. If we let it build up too much, it will burst like a balloon. Better to let the air out slowly instead.

Releasing our anger slowly is part of processing it appropriately. We need to accept that it's there, recognize that it has a purpose, and work through it until we're able to let it go. We'll need to be both prayerful and patient. We may need to confront those who have hurt us and challenge their behavior, and we'll need to mourn whatever we've lost through our being hurt: be it a relationship, a dream, time and energy, or something tangible that was stolen, lost, or destroyed.

To let go of our anger entirely, it's essential that we forgive the cause of our anger. That may seem hard to do, especially when our anger is intense. But forgiveness is a decision, and we can always choose to forgive, even when our anger is white-hot. The more we delay that choice, the more stuck in anger we'll become.

Popular culture insists: "Don't get mad; get even." Jesus assures us that it's okay to get mad. He insists, however, that we not get even. He also insists that we forgive. To do that, we need to work through our anger. Father Lawrence Jenco, who forgave the Lebanese Shiite Muslim terrorists who kidnapped him in 1985, knew this well. "Unless we allow ourselves to feel the pain," he wrote, "it is unlikely an act of forgiveness will be genuine."

CHAPTER 21

Let's Talk About It

When Timothy McVeigh bombed the Oklahoma City federal building in 1995, Bud Welch's daughter, Julie, was inside. Bud was planning on having lunch with Julie that day, but she never made it. Along with 167 others, she died in the blast.

Bud Welch was devastated at the loss of his daughter. He began to drink heavily and to smoke three packs of cigarettes a day. Often he'd wander down to a tree that overlooked the site of where the federal building had stood. There he thought of Julie, his heart filled with sadness and anger. Over time, however, he came to realize that he was sick. He questioned whether or not he needed retribution, and he explored how to move forward in his life.

Bud eventually understood that the rage that filled him was the same as the rage that led to his daughter's death, and that it had to end with him. Drawing upon his

Catholic faith, he forgave Timothy McVeigh and began to speak publicly about the necessity of forgiveness.

Since that time, Bud has testified before multiple state legislatures, the British and European Parliaments, the Russian Duma, and the U.S. House Judiciary Committee. He's written for newspapers and journals big and small, including *Time* and *Newsweek*, and he's appeared on major television shows such as *60 Minutes, Larry King Live, Dateline NBC,* and *The Today Show.* In the process, Bud has inspired countless lives through his personal witness.

Not surprisingly, many people who want to forgive approach Bud Welch for help. They're moved by his testimony, and they hope that they can learn to forgive as he came to forgive Timothy McVeigh. They appreciate that only someone who has traveled down the road of forgiveness understands their thoughts and feelings. Only someone who has shared their experience of pain and loss can point them in the right direction. For his part, Bud is happy to lend a hand.

In order to forgive, we often need another's help; someone with whom we can talk it through. We don't always realize that, however, and we keep our struggle to ourselves. Maybe we're embarrassed or ashamed about the situation in which we were hurt. Perhaps we're private and hesitant to share deep feelings or personal experiences. It could be we're convinced that seeking another's help is a sign of weakness. We think, "Can't just God and I handle it together?"

Perhaps. But remember: Christianity is not just "Jesus and me." It's also "Jesus and we." Christians form a body, the body of Christ. As St. Paul describes it, Christ is the head of that body and we, the baptized, are members. Jesus expects the members of his body to help and support one another, and he will sometimes use the hands of one member to extend his own healing touch to another.

That's why, should we ask Jesus for the grace to forgive, he may very well send someone across our path to help us. It might be someone we already know; then again, it might be a complete stranger. Either way, this person will have already learned to forgive, and will be prepared to share that experience with us, just as Bud Welch did.

When faced with an opportunity to forgive another, we can easily fool ourselves. We're often not objective or rational when we're hurt or angry. We make excuses why we shouldn't or can't forgive, or we simply get stuck in our bitterness and rage. That's when we need the assistance of someone who can see things more clearly. As St. John Climacus observed, "God has arranged that no one can see his own faults as clearly as his neighbor does!" We don't need a yes-man who tells us what we want to hear, even if well-intentioned and sympathetic to our pain. We may need a shoulder to cry upon, but we don't need an enabler who validates our bitterness. We need someone who has our true best interests in mind, someone who loves us enough to speak the truth, even if the truth may hurt.

Whoever those persons may be, we need to trust them to lead us where we need to go. Sometimes they may hold our hand. Sometimes they'll drag us kicking and screaming. Sometimes they'll push us forward from behind. At times, they might be our cheerleaders, giving us encouragement. At other times, they may have to shake us out of our self-pity. Over the course of time, they may need to do all of the above.

To have a need to "talk it through" is not a license to gossip about the one who has hurt us. Everyone has a right to a good name and reputation. We shouldn't defame another or conduct a smear campaign to get sympathy or make people choose sides. It's tempting to do this, however. We'll say to a friend, "You really need to know what this person is like." We pretend to be concerned for our friend's welfare, but we're really trying to get our friend to dislike that person as much as we do. It's for good reason that Christians joke about presenting "dirty laundry" as a prayer intention!

That's why, in sharing our struggle, we need to choose a partner who, in addition to being wise, is trustworthy and discreet. He or she might be a family member, a friend, or someone we've met in church circles. It could be a minister on our parish staff, or a priest with whom we make a regular confession. A professional therapist who honors our faith commitment can help us greatly too, especially if we've been suffering from depression or post-traumatic stress disorder (PTSD).

St. Bernard of Clairvaux wrote, "Whoever makes himself his own guide, becomes the disciple of a fool." Hard words, but sadly true. On our faith journey, it's best not to travel alone. Jesus sent off his disciples in pairs for mutual support. We, too, need support on our journey, especially when we're called to forgive. When it comes to forgiving from the *heart*, we might say that two *heads* are better than one.

CHAPTER 22

Keep on Keeping On

It was meant to be a friendly hunting expedition between cousins. Christophe de Chantal and M. D'Anlezy rode off together on horseback, their guns loaded and ready. One of those guns would find a target. That target, however, was not the one intended. In a tragic accident, D'Anlezy shot Christophe in the upper leg, inflicting a serious wound. The year was 1601. Christophe was thirty-seven years old and the father of four young children. His wife of nine years, twenty-eight-year-old Jane de Chantal, was at home at the time of the accident.

Christophe suffered horribly for nine days. Surgeons only made matters worse. Understandably, his cousin was deeply distressed over what had happened, but Christophe reassured D'Anlezy, insisting that the accident could have happened to anyone. "Dear cousin, dear friend," he said, "it just happened; it wasn't your fault. I beg you, don't commit the sin of hating yourself when you haven't done anything wrong." Christophe forgave D'Anlezy and even had a mention of his pardon inscribed in the records of his parish church, so that no one would later prosecute his cousin. Shortly thereafter, Christophe died in Jane's arms.[23]

Christophe had urged Jane to forgive D'Anlezy as well, but she could not. After Christophe's death, she sank into a deep depression. For fourth months she secluded herself and neglected her children. She would not permit D'Anlezy's name to be mentioned in her presence. Her grief was so intense that her health began to suffer. Nevertheless, Jane held on to her Catholic faith and prayed for a spiritual director. God granted her wish in the Bishop of Geneva, whom we know today as St. Francis de Sales.

Francis soon became aware that Jane had a need to forgive D'Anlezy, but, in his gentleness and wisdom, he knew that forgiveness would require time and patience. Members of Jane's family wanted to rush her along, but Francis knew better. With Francis's guidance and encouragement, Jane slowly came to forgive D'Anlezy. After having avoided him for years, she found herself willing to greet him in the street. Next, she managed to invite him to her house. Finally, D'Anlezy asked her to be the godmother of his newborn child. Overwhelmed with emotion, Jane burst into tears, but accepted his invitation. She had now completely forgiven D'Anlezy, six years after Christophe's death. Jane would be declared a saint 143 years later.

Some may find it puzzling that one who became a saint would have taken so long to forgive, but St. Jane de Chantal's experience makes it quite clear that forgiveness can be hard even for the most devout persons. If forgiveness came naturally to us, this wouldn't be the case. Forgiveness, however, does not come naturally to any human being. As Pope John Paul II explained, forgiveness goes "against the natural instinct to pay back evil for evil."

For forgiveness to take time is perfectly normal. Forgiveness is a decision, but it's also a process, because we often have to make the same decision to forgive over and over again. Jesus taught us to forgive one who wrongs us "seventy times seven times" (Mt 18:22). We typically understand this as meaning that we need to repeatedly forgive someone who hurts us multiple times, but it also means that we may have to forgive someone multiple times for the same offense! We make the decision to forgive and experience some peace, but then resentment or a desire for revenge flares up again, and we find ourselves having to forgive once more.

St. Paul instructs us to not let the sun go down on our anger (see Eph 4:26). We may try to honor his words and go to bed thinking that we've forgiven. When we wake up in the morning, however, the memory of our hurt fills our mind again, and we're back to square one. Ancient Christian writers referred to these thoughts as "morning demons." They can be terribly persistent. C. S. Lewis once wrote,

> There is no use in talking as if forgiveness were easy. We all know the old joke, "You've given up smoking once; I've given it up a dozen times." In the same way I could say of a certain man, "Have I forgiven him for what he did that day? I've forgiven him more times than I can count." For we find that the work of forgiveness has to be done over and over again.[24]

Forgiving a deep hurt typically requires passing through different stages such as denial, anger, bargaining, depression, and acceptance, as described by Elizabeth Kübler-Ross. When in denial, we avoid our pain through shocked disbelief. "This really can't be happening to me!" we insist. But eventually the pain will be felt. Anger will surface. Temptations to revenge or retaliate may arise. We bargain by making excuses for why we can't or shouldn't have to forgive. Depression may follow. We shed tears, mourn what's been lost, retreat into a shell, blame ourselves for what happened. Hopefully, however, all this is ultimately replaced by acceptance, forgiveness, and peace. All these different stages don't happen in a neat progression. And not everyone will experience all of them. But everyone will experience some of them.

The hard work of forgiveness can be frustrating and discouraging, but there's grace to be found in the struggle. The tragedy is not that we find ourselves wrestling with powerfully negative thoughts or feelings. We can't flip a switch and turn off those emotions overnight. We may never be free of them entirely. The real tragedy is to throw in the towel and simply give up trying.

When forgiving seems like the last thing we want to do, or should be asked to do, it helps to hold on to the thought that forgiveness is a duty. That's what Terry Anderson did. An Associated Press journalist, he was captured and held hostage by terrorists in Lebanon for seven years. He suffered greatly. His captors "did great harm to me and my family," he later wrote. Forgiveness didn't come easily. But thanks to a gift of a Bible and the encouragement of a fellow captive who was a priest, Anderson slowly found the strength to forgive. "I am a

Christian and a Catholic, and I must forgive," he insisted, "no matter how hard that may be."[25]

Terry Anderson's experience shows us that, when it comes to forgiving, sometimes we just need to "keep on keeping on." Jesus understands that well. In his love for us, he gave us a commandment to forgive. What he didn't give us was a deadline.

CHAPTER 23

Check Your Pulse

Under the Ayatollah Khomeini, life for Christians in Iran was extremely difficult. Christian institutions were forcibly closed, property was confiscated, and Christian leaders were harassed and jailed. Christians even became targets of violence. Late one night in 1980, intruders broke into the home of Bishop Hassan Dehqani-Tafti, the Anglican Bishop of Tehran. They burst into his wife Margaret's bedroom and fired five shots. One hit her in the hand, but the other four missed, striking her pillow instead. Margaret recovered, but she and Bishop Hassan left Iran for safety in England.

Their son, Bahram, chose to remain in his native country, a decision that would prove fatal. While returning home one night after teaching English at Tehran University, his car was ambushed by government agents, and Bahram was shot and killed. Because his parents were living in exile, they were unable to attend his funeral.

However, Bishop Hassan composed a beautiful prayer for the liturgy that concluded with these words:

> *O God,*
> *Our son's blood has multiplied the fruit*
>   *of the Spirit in our souls;*
> *So when his murderers stand before Thee*
>   *on the day of judgment*
> *Remember the fruit of the Spirit by which*
>   *they have enriched our lives,*
> *And forgive.*[26]

After Bishop Hassan himself died, one newspaper obituary described him as a "man of gentle and compassionate spirit" who "seemed incapable of thinking evil of anyone."[27] Nevertheless, for even such a holy person to forgive his son's assassins at his funeral is a remarkable thing indeed. Publicly hoping for their salvation is more astounding still.

To express such a hope is a powerful sign that one has truly forgiven. There are other signs as well. Whenever we're striving to forgive another, it's good to look for these signs. We should reflect on our actions and attitudes to determine if we're making any progress. We need to "check our pulse," if you will, to see how we're doing.

As with Bishop Hassan, a strong indication that we've forgiven is revealed in our hope for our offender's ultimate fate. To put it bluntly, would we want them to "go to heaven" or would we rather that they "go to hell?" When life gets hard, it's natural, and even appropriate, for us to be consoled and encouraged by the thought of a heavenly reward, but when others are responsible for making our life hard, it's tempting to imagine, in a smug sort of way, that one day they'll get what's coming to them. We'll be blessed for all eternity and, well, they won't. Our imaginary "heaven" will be filled with what in German is called *schadenfreude*: delight over another's suffering, downfall, or misfortune.

St. Augustine once described heaven as characterized by light, rest, happiness, and peace. Gloating was not on his list. Given that, we should take stock of what we hope will be the final end of those we need to forgive: Do we wish them to share the light, rest, happiness, and peace we long for? Or would we prefer they endure the opposite? Would we rather they have paradise, or perdition? Should we choose the latter, it appears that we still have work to do on forgiveness.

Perhaps we wouldn't want the one who hurt us to be denied heaven. As the old saying goes, we "wouldn't wish that on our worst enemy." Even so, some of our actions may reveal that we've not yet completely forgiven, even if our thoughts are generally in the right place. For instance, how do we act toward those who have hurt us, should we encounter them? Are we civil and polite, or are we cold, unkind, or passive-aggressive? Do we slander or spread nasty rumors about them? Or can we bite our lip or even say something positive about them? Do we pray for them?

We should check our feelings too, to determine how well we're doing with forgiveness. Do bitterness and anger still eat away at us? Does part of us still want revenge? And if we still feel the pain despite all our best efforts to forgive, do we try to numb it with food, alcohol, irresponsible sex, or some other negative behavior?

Or, on the other hand, do we experience a measure of peace? Can we encounter this certain person in a social gathering without our feathers being ruffled or our blood pressure rising?

Another sign that we've forgiven is an ability to look back at the hurtful situation and find things for which to be thankful. At the time, we may have thought that God was absent or that he didn't care. But now, we can see God's hand in that situation and appreciate that he allowed it to help us grow. We now understand an occasion of pain as an occasion of grace and an opportunity to forgive. It made us stronger Christians. It taught us something about ourselves, about others, and about God. We learned to rely more completely upon God. We responded to hate with love. We witnessed to Christ.

In his funeral prayer for Bahram, Bishop Hassan thanked God for many things. He expressed gratitude for the opportunity to follow in the footsteps of Jesus's suffering, an understanding that such an ordeal "burns up all selfishness and possessiveness in us," and that Bahram's violent death "makes obvious as never before our need to trust in God's love."[28]

Jesus himself "learned obedience from what he suffered" from others (Heb 5:8). We can learn many things through our suffering; being grateful for those lessons is a strong indication we've forgiven those who caused that suffering. In other words, forgiveness allows us to thank God for our pain in addition to our joy. Scottish poet George Matheson (1842–1906) put this well:

> My God, I have never thanked Thee for my thorn. I
> have thanked Thee a thousand times for my roses, but

, not once for my thorn. I have been looking forward to a world where I shall get compensation for my cross, but I have never thought of my cross as a present glory. . . . [T]each me the glory of the cross; teach me the value of my thorn. Show me that I have climbed to Thee by the path of pain. Show me that my tears have made my rainbow.

CHAPTER 24

The Choice Is Ours

We were standing in a darkened church. Sunday Masses were over, the crowds had gone home, and the lights had been shut off. The only illumination came from the gentle flickering of dozens of votive candles: red under the statue of St. Joseph, blue in the little shrine to Mary. They'd all been lit by worshipers as they offered a prayer. The pastor and I paused as we gazed upon them in silence. After a long moment, he turned to me and said, "You know, every one of those candles represents a broken heart." I had to agree. Perhaps a handful had been lit in thanksgiving for blessings received, but most of them signified a cry for help.

Life is a wonderful gift from God. At times, however, life can seem anything but wonderful. Like death and taxes, suffering is inevitable; it's simply part of the human condition. We fallen human beings hurt one another, and we hurt ourselves. Some more, some less, but we all do.

It's for good reason that the ancient Catholic prayer, the *Salve Regina*, describes our journey through this world as through a "valley of tears."

As Christians, however, Jesus calls us to add love to this tear-stained world, especially in those places where love seems most absent. We are to be the "light of the world" in the midst of its darkness. We all want this world to be a more loving place, but sometimes it's up to us to make it so. As St. John of the Cross taught, "Where there is no love, put love, and you will find love."

Such love involves forgiveness. Forgiveness is a gesture of love we offer to God's glory, as a blessing to others, and for the sake of our own health, happiness, and holiness. Like love, true forgiveness isn't concerned with fairness. Fairness requires strict justice. But with forgiveness, justice is tempered by mercy and inspired by grace. As has often been said, "Justice is getting what you deserve. Mercy is not getting what you deserve. Grace is getting what you don't deserve." Forgiveness isn't deserved. It's a free gift; others don't have to earn it. Consider the words on a wall of Mother Teresa's Calcutta home for children: "People are often unreasonable, illogical, self-centered. Forgive them anyway. You see, in the final analysis, it is between you and God. It was never between you and them anyway!"

The God who calls us to forgive pours out his forgiveness upon us with generosity. An old tale from one of the Desert Fathers, hermits of the ancient Egyptian desert, illustrates this well.

> Abba Mios was asked by a soldier whether God would forgive a sinner. After instructing him at some length, the old man asked him, "Tell me, my dear, if your

cloak were torn, would you throw it away?" "Oh no!" he replied. "I would mend it and wear it again." The old man said to him: "Well, if you care for your cloak, will not God show mercy to his own creature?"[29]

Just as the soldier would mend his torn cloak, so God mends us. He heals our brokenness, forgives our sins, then sends us forth to heal and forgive others. If we don't, we'll likely stay stuck in resentment. Psychologist M. Scott Peck once likened this to a game of Monopoly that seems to drag on forever. We want it to stop, but then we pass Go, collect our $200, and keep right on playing. The only way to end the game is for us to put our foot down and say, "I don't want to do this anymore! I quit playing!" Stopping the resentment game is called forgiveness.[30]

And forgiveness is tough. It's contrary to our fallen human nature and it requires humility, courage, risk, and perseverance. But if we refuse to forgive, we contribute to the world's sorrow (and there's enough of that already); we demonize the persons who wronged us (and that's unfair to them); and we deny ourselves the gift of God's forgiveness (which is foolishness to us).

The folly of refusing to forgive dawned upon the English poet Rosamund Herklots while she pulled weeds in her nephew's garden. Just as weeds choke life out of a garden, she concluded, so do bitterness and resentment choke life out of us.[31] Inspired by this insight, she went on to write what would become a popular hymn:

"Forgive our sins as we forgive,"
 you taught us, Lord, to pray,
But you alone can grant us grace

to live the words we say.
How can your pardon reach
*   and bless the unforgiving heart,*
That broods on wrongs and will not let
*   old bitterness depart?*
In blazing light your cross reveals
*   the truth we dimly knew:*
What trivial debts are owed to us,
*   how great our debt to you!*
Lord, cleanse the depths within our souls
*   and bid resentment cease.*
Then, bound to all in bonds of love,
*   our lives will spread your peace.*[32]

There are times when forgiving may be the last thing we want to do. We might try to convince ourselves that, for whatever reason, we don't need to forgive, but that's taking the short view. Jesus, who offers us everlasting happiness with him, invites us to take the long view. We should consider: At the end of our life, what kind of person do we want to be as we step into eternity? Bitter and resentful? Or peaceful and forgiving? Better yet, when faced with the decision to forgive, we can take St. Ignatius Loyola's suggestion and ask ourselves: When I face the Lord at the end of my life, what choice will I wish I'd made? As followers of Jesus, there's only one decision we can make: the decision to forgive.

When we've been hurt, we may feel as if we're surrounded by darkness. Perhaps we'll light a candle in our church as we cry to God for help, but there's another candle we can light, too. An old Chinese proverb says, "It's better to light a candle than to curse the darkness."

That's good advice. Don't curse your darkness, but scatter your gloom with the light of forgiveness: for you, for others, for God.

A Final Word . . .
About Where to Begin

Forgiveness may be understood as a journey. It has a starting point (our experience of hurt) and a destination (achieving forgiveness). If we've not made this journey before, we may need some help on the way. If this describes you, consider the steps below. To complete our journey, we'll need to take each one of them.

Step One: Turn Toward God

The forgiveness journey begins with our making a turn, a turn toward God. It's only when we face him that we'll be able to face our pain.

God wants to be our traveling companion on this journey, and he doesn't want us to travel in silence. We need to speak with him and ask for help and healing, patience and courage, wisdom and strength. What we say to God may change over the course of the journey. We may begin by saying "Help me," but end by saying "Thank you."

Step Two: Don't Get Stuck

Feeling angry when we've been hurt is no sin. God gave us the capacity for anger. What we do with that anger, however, can make or break our journey of forgiveness.

If our anger hardens into bitterness and resentment, or leads us to seek retaliation or revenge, we'll be stuck in our anger. On the other hand, our anger can move us forward. It can lead us to confront an injustice, defend ourselves, or challenge the one who hurt us. Anger and love can go hand-in-hand.

Tell God if you feel angry with him. Our anger may reveal a lack of faith and trust. But God always meets us where we are; he doesn't rush ahead and wait for us to catch up. God is always at our side on this journey—even if we have a long way to go.

Step Three: Choose the Narrow Way

Forgiveness is a decision, not a feeling. When we've been hurt, we may feel angry, sad, frustrated, confused, or scared, and that's okay. But in spite of our feelings, we can still choose to forgive, to avoid retaliation, and to do what love requires.

On the journey of forgiveness, we'll encounter a crossroads. We can choose the way of resentment and retaliation or we can choose the way of forgiveness and peace. The way of forgiveness may be the more narrow and difficult path. But it's the only one that will lead us to where we ultimately want to be.

Step Four: Avoid Danger

The way of forgiveness is often hard. But that doesn't mean we can't steer clear of unnecessary hardships or outright danger. If you're a victim of violence or serious abuse, walk away—or run if you have to. Jesus himself avoided danger many times.

Jesus did suffer, but only when it was necessary to fulfill God's plan for his life. Carrying a cross was part of his journey. We'll carry crosses, too. But not all suffering is a cross Jesus wants us to carry. Some suffering we're meant to avoid.

Step Five: Stop into Church

On any long, hard journey, we'll need both nourishment for strength and healing for when we're weary and wounded. On the journey of forgiveness, Jesus offers us both. In the sacrament of Reconciliation, he forgives and heals the wounds of our sins, so we might give what we have been given. In the Eucharist, he nourishes us with the food and drink of his Body and Blood. He gives us grace to carry on, and then he sends us forth in peace to love and to forgive.

Step Six: Ask for Directions

We're not the first to make the journey of forgiveness. Those who have gone before us can help us on our way. We should ask directions from such a person. He or she might be a wise and trusted friend, a brother or sister in Christ, a priest, deacon, or other minister, or a professional counselor. God knows we need such help. He may send someone to cross our path to keep us on that path. Sometimes they'll walk alongside us. At other times they'll push us from behind or even drag us onward.

Step Seven: Lighten Your Load

When he first sent out his disciples, Jesus instructed them to travel lightly. On the journey of forgiveness, we need to travel lightly too. To do that, we may need to shed some baggage. We can unload paralyzing guilt by seeking God's forgiveness, and we can unburden ourselves of any unreasonable expectations we've placed on the one we're trying to forgive.

Step Eight: Look over Your Shoulder

As we journey toward forgiveness, it helps to look back to the time when we were hurt and evaluate what happened. Were we in any way responsible? Did we do something, or fail to do something, that contributed to the circumstances? What about the persons who hurt us? What have their lifes' journeys been like? What factors have led them to become who they are or to do what they do? Understanding their brokenness can help us forgive their contributions to ours.

Step Nine: Don't Turn Back

Forgiveness isn't a sprint; it's a marathon. It's a long, hard journey, and we can't expect to reach our destination quickly. At times, we may feel like giving up. It may seem like we're taking one step forward and two steps back! But we need to keep on keeping on and persevere in putting one foot in front of the other. Consider Jesus: he pressed on to Jerusalem, knowing that there he would carry the cross—and then be nailed to it. But he knew also that his journey would end in Resurrection. There's hope for the end of our journey, too.

Step Ten: Journey's End

Our journey's destination is forgiveness. But how do we know if we've arrived? Our thoughts, actions, and feelings will tell us if we're getting closer. It may be that our journey of forgiveness will not be complete until our life's journey is complete. It's good to imagine that day, however, and consider the choices we must make to be the type of person we'll want to be when we meet Jesus face to face.

Until then, we can hope that our final end, and the final end of the one who hurt us, will be one and the same. That's what Jesus wants, and so should we.

Notes

1. Peter John Cameron, OP, "Editorial," *Magnificat*, March 2000, p. 1.

2. "Forgive Their Trespasses," http://www.webmd.com/balance/features/forgive-their-trespasses, June 18, 2001.

3. Priit J. Vesilind, "Oil and Honor at Pearl Harbor," *National Geographic*, June 2001, pp. 98–99.

4. Roxanne Roberts, "To Forgive, Divine: The Wisdom, and Healthfulness, of Letting Go of Anger," *The Washington Post*, March 31, 2002, p. F05.

5. Lisa Collier Cool, "The Power of Forgiving: Best Way to Heal a Heart," *Reader's Digest*, May 2004, pp. 91–93.

6. Beth Griffin, "Rwandan Says God Saved Her from Genocide to Be Witness to Forgiveness," Catholic News Service, November 15, 2007.

7. Craig S. Keener, *A Commentary on the Gospel of Matthew* (Grand Rapids, MI: W. B. Eerdmans, 1999), pp. 456–461.

8. David Van Biema, "Should All Be Forgiven?" *Time*, March 28, 1999.

9. Peter John Cameron, OP, "Editorial," *Magnificat*, March 2000, pp. 1–2.

10. Gary Washburn, "Palmiero Back to Baseball After Hearing," MLB.com, March 18, 2005.

11. John L. Allen, Jr., "A Sicilian Lesson in the Complex Bond Between Bishops and Saints," *National Catholic Reporter*, December 14, 2006.

12. Corrie ten Boom, *Tramp for the Lord* (Fort Washington, PA: Christian Literature Crusade), 1974.

13. John Monbourquette, *How to Forgive: A Step-by-Step Guide* (Cincinnati, OH: St. Anthony Messenger Press, 2000), pp. 152–153.

14. Dan Barry, "2 Lives: Attack, Injury, Hope, Death; Officer Forgave Troubled Youth Who Shot Him," *New York Times*, September 14, 1995.

15. John Burger, "Hero Cop: Detective McDonald Urges Youth to Forgive, Frequent the Sacraments," *Catholic New York*, 1998.

16. Michael Morris, OP, "Saint John of God," *Magnificat*, issue unknown, pp. I–VI.

17. Henri J. M. Nouwen, *Home Tonight* (New York: Doubleday, 2009), p. 105.

18. Gregory Popcak and Lisa Popcak, *Parenting with Grace: Catholic Parents' Guide to Raising Almost Perfect Kids* (Huntington, IN: Our Sunday Visitor, 2000), pp. 22–23.

19. Dorotheos of Gaza, *Discourses and Sayings*. Translated by Eric P. Wheeler (Kalamazoo, MI: Cistercian Publications, 1977), p. 134.

20. Jude Winkler, O.F.M. Conv., *Handbook for Proclaimers of the Word, Liturgical Year C, 2007* (Totowa, NJ: Catholic Book Publishing Corporation, 2006), pp. 224–225.

21. Andrew Romano, "Truth Is, I'm the Same Guy I Always Was," *Newsweek*, June 11, 2007, pp. 51–55.

22. William Barclay, *The Gospel of Mark, Daily Bible Study Revised Edition* (Philadelphia: The Westminster Press, 1975), pp. 273–275.

23. Vincent J. O'Malley, *Ordinary Suffering of Extraordinary Saints* (Huntington, IN: Our Sunday Visitor, 2000), pp. 34–35.

24. C. S. Lewis, *Reflections on the Psalms* (New York: Harvest / Harcourt, 1958), pp. 24–25.

25. James Elliott, O.F.M. Conv., *The Freedom of Forgiveness*, Good News Notes, No. 33 (Ellicott City, MD: The Companions of St. Anthony, 1998).

26. Hassan B. Dehqani-Tafti, *The Hard Awakening* (New York: Seabury Press, 1981).

27. "The Rt. Rev. Hassan Dehqani-Tafti," *The Daily Telegraph*, May 1, 2008, Obituaries.

28. Hassan B. Dehqani-Tafti, *The Hard Awakening* (New York: Seabury Press, 1981), pp. 113–114.

29. Yushi Nomura, *Desert Wisdom: Sayings from the Desert Fathers* (Maryknoll, NY: Orbis Books, 2001), p. 11.

30. M. Scott Peck, *Further Along the Road Less Travelled* (New York: Simon and Schuster, 1993), p. 40.

31. Raymond F. Glover, ed., *The Hymnal 1982 Companion* (New York: Church Hymnal Corporation, 1995), p. 1245.

32. Text: Rosamond Herklots, b. 1905, © Oxford University Press.

Acknowledgments

"Forgive our sins, as we forgive" by Rosamond Herklots (1905–1987). Reproduced by permission of Oxford University Press. All rights reserved.

Excerpts from *Tramp for the Lord* © 1972 by Guideposts Magazine, New York, NY 10016. All rights reserved.

Excerpt from *Discourses and Sayings* by Dorotheos of Gaza © 1977 by Cistercian Publications, 2008, by Order of Saint Benedict, Inc. Published by Liturgical Press, Collegeville, MN. Reprinted with permission.

Excerpt from editorial by Fr. Peter John Cameron, OP. Reprinted from MAGNIFICAT, March 2000, No. 16, pp. 2–3. With permission of Magnificat® U.S.A., LLC. To order call 1-866-273-5215. Web site: www.magnificat.com. All rights reserved.

Excerpt from *Reflections on the Psalms*, © 1958 by C. S. Lewis, renewed 1986 by Arthur Owen Barfield, reprinted by permission of Harcourt, Inc. *Reflections on the Psalms* by C. S. Lewis © C. S. Lewis Pte. Ltd. 1958. Extract reprinted by permission.

Excerpt from "Rwandan Says God Saved Her from Genocide to Be Witness to Forgiveness" by Beth Griffin © 2007, Catholic News Service, www.CatholicNews.com. Used with permission of CNS.

BOOKS & MEDIA

A mission of the Daughters of St. Paul

As apostles of Jesus Christ, evangelizing today's world:

We are CALLED to holiness
by God's living Word and Eucharist.

We COMMUNICATE the Gospel message
through our lives and through all
available forms of media.

We SERVE the Church
by responding to the hopes and needs
of all people with the Word of God,
in the spirit of St. Paul.

For more information visit our Web site:
www.pauline.org.

BOOKS & MEDIA

The Daughters of St. Paul operate book and media centers at the following addresses. Visit, call or write the one nearest you today, or find us on the World Wide Web, www.pauline.org

CALIFORNIA

3908 Sepulveda Blvd, Culver City, CA 90230	310-397-8676
935 Brewster Avenue, Redwood City, CA 94063	650-369-4230
5945 Balboa Avenue, San Diego, CA 92111	858-565-9181

FLORIDA

145 S.W. 107th Avenue, Miami, FL 33174	305-559-6715

HAWAII

1143 Bishop Street, Honolulu, HI 96813	808-521-2731
Neighbor Islands call:	866-521-2731

ILLINOIS

172 North Michigan Avenue, Chicago, IL 60601	312-346-4228

LOUISIANA

4403 Veterans Memorial Blvd, Metairie, LA 70006	504-887-7631

MASSACHUSETTS

885 Providence Hwy, Dedham, MA 02026	781-326-5385

MISSOURI

9804 Watson Road, St. Louis, MO 63126	314-965-3512

NEW YORK

64 West 38th Street, New York, NY 10018	212-754-1110

PENNSYLVANIA

Philadelphia—relocating	215-676-9494

SOUTH CAROLINA

243 King Street, Charleston, SC 29401	843-577-0175

VIRGINIA

1025 King Street, Alexandria, VA 22314	703-549-3806

CANADA

3022 Dufferin Street, Toronto, ON M6B 3T5	416-781-9131

¡También somos su fuente para libros,
videos y música en español!